Joyce Appleby on *Thomas Jefferson*
Louis Auchincloss on *Theodore Roosevelt*
Jean Baker on *James Buchanan*
H. W. Brands on *Woodrow Wilson*
Douglas Brinkley on *Gerald Ford*
James MacGregor Burns and Susan Dunn on *George Washington*
Robert Dallek on *James Monroe*
John W. Dean on *Warren Harding*
John Patrick Diggins on *John Adams*
E. L. Doctorow on *Abraham Lincoln*
Henry F. Graff on *Grover Cleveland*
Roy Jenkins on *Franklin Delano Roosevelt*
Zachary Karabell on *Chester A. Arthur*
William E. Leuchtenburg on *Herbert Hoover*
Robert V. Remini on *John Quincy Adams*
John Seigenthaler on *James K. Polk*
Hans L. Trefousse on *Rutherford B. Hayes*
Tom Wicker on *Dwight D. Eisenhower*
Ted Widmer on *Martin Van Buren*
Sean Wilentz on *Andrew Jackson*
Garry Wills on *James Madison*

ALSO BY ROBERT V. REMINI

Andrew Jackson: Volume One
The Course of American Empire, 1767–1821

Andrew Jackson: Volume Two
The Course of American Freedom, 1822–1832

Andrew Jackson: Volume Three
The Course of American Democracy, 1833–1845

The Jacksonian Era

Daniel Webster: The Man and His Time

Henry Clay: Statesman for the Union

The Election of Andrew Jackson

Andrew Jackson and the Bank War

The Legacy of Andrew Jackson

Martin Van Buren and the Making of the Democratic Party

The Battle of New Orleans

Andrew Jackson and His Indian Wars

John Quincy Adams

Robert V. Remini

John Quincy Adams

THE AMERICAN PRESIDENTS

ARTHUR M. SCHLESINGER, JR., GENERAL EDITOR

Times Books

HENRY HOLT AND COMPANY, NEW YORK

For HUGH VAN DUSEN and WENDY WOLF,
wonderful friends and superb editors

Times Books
Henry Holt and Company, LLC
Publishers since 1866
115 West 18th Street
New York, New York 10011

LIBRARY OF CONGRESS CATALOGING-IN-PUBLICATION DATA
Remini, Robert Vincent, 1921–
    John Quincy Adams / Robert V. Remini—1st ed.
    p. cm.—(The American presidents series)
Includes bibliographical references (p.) and index.
ISBN: 0-8050-6939-9
    1. Adams, John Quincy, 1767–1848. 2. Presidents—United States—Biography.
3. United States—Politics and government—1825–1829. 4. United States—
Politics and government—1789–1815. I. Title. II. American presidents series
(Times Books (Firm))
E377.R46 2002
973.5'2'092—dc21
[B]   2002024210

First Edition 2002

Printed in the United States of America
1 3 5 7 9 10 8 6 4 2

Contents

Editor's Note   xiii

1. A Privileged Young Man   1
2. Finding a Career   19
3. From Federalist to Republican   33
4. Secretary of State   50
5. The Election of 1824–25   62
6. "The Perilous Experiment"   75
7. Indian Removal   88
8. Diplomatic Successes and Failures   101
9. The Tariff of Abominations   109
10. "Skunks of Party Slander"   117
11. Congressman John Quincy Adams   130
12. Victory!   146

Notes   157
Milestones   161
Bibliography   165
Index   167

Editor's Note

THE AMERICAN PRESIDENCY

The president is the central player in the American political order. That would seem to contradict the intentions of the Founding Fathers. Remembering the horrid example of the British monarchy, they invented a separation of powers in order, as Justice Brandeis later put it, "to preclude the exercise of arbitrary power." Accordingly, they divided the government into three allegedly equal and coordinate branches—the executive, the legislative, and the judiciary.

But a system based on the tripartite separation of powers has an inherent tendency toward inertia and stalemate. One of the three branches must take the initiative if the system is to move. The executive branch alone is structurally capable of taking that initiative. The Founders must have sensed this when they accepted Alexander Hamilton's proposition in the Seventieth Federalist that "energy in the executive is a leading character in the definition of good government." They thus envisaged a strong president—but within an equally strong system of constitutional accountability. (The term *imperial presidency* arose in the 1970s to describe the situation when the balance between power and accountability is upset in favor of the executive.)

The American system of self-government thus comes to focus in the presidency—"the vital place of action in the system," as Woodrow Wilson put it. Henry Adams, himself the great-grandson and grandson of presidents as well as the most brilliant of American historians, said that the American president "resembles the commander of a ship at sea. He must have a helm to grasp, a course to steer, a port to seek." The men in the White House (thus far only men, alas) in steering their chosen courses have shaped our destiny as a nation.

Biography offers an easy education in American history, rendering the past more human, more vivid, more intimate, more accessible, more connected to ourselves. Biography reminds us that presidents are not supermen. They are human beings too, worrying about decisions, attending to wives and children, juggling balls in the air, and putting on their pants one leg at a time. Indeed, as Emerson contended, "There is properly no history; only biography."

Presidents serve us as inspirations, and they also serve us as warnings. They provide bad examples as well as good. The nation, the Supreme Court has said, has "no right to expect that it will always have wise and humane rulers, sincerely attached to the principles of the Constitution. Wicked men, ambitious of power, with hatred of liberty and contempt of law, may fill the place once occupied by Washington and Lincoln."

The men in the White House express the ideal and the values, the frailties and the flaws, of the voters who send them there. It is altogether natural that we should want to know more about the virtues and the vices of the fellows we have elected to govern us. As we know more about them, we will know more about ourselves. The French political philosopher Joseph de Maistre said, "Every nation has the government it deserves."

At the start of the twenty-first century, forty-two men have made it to the Oval Office. (George W. Bush is counted our forty-third president, because Grover Cleveland, who served nonconsecutive terms, is counted twice.) Of the parade of presidents, a dozen or so lead the polls periodically conducted by historians and political scientists. What makes a great president?

Great presidents possess, or are possessed by, a vision of an ideal America. Their passion, as they grasp the helm, is to set the ship of state on the right course toward the port they seek. Great presidents also have a deep psychic connection with the needs, anxieties, dreams of people. "I do not believe," said Wilson, "that any man can lead who does not act . . . under the impulse of a profound sympathy with those whom he leads—a sympathy which is insight—an insight which is of the heart rather than of the intellect."

"All of our great presidents," said Franklin D. Roosevelt, "were leaders of thought at a time when certain ideas in the life of the nation had to be clarified." So Washington incarnated the idea of federal union, Jefferson and Jackson the idea of democracy, Lincoln union and freedom, Cleveland rugged honesty. Theodore Roosevelt and Wilson, said FDR, were both "moral leaders, each in his own way and his own time, who used the presidency as a pulpit."

To succeed, presidents must not only have a port to seek but they must convince Congress and the electorate that it is a port worth seeking. Politics in a democracy is ultimately an educational process, an adventure in persuasion and consent. Every president stands in Theodore Roosevelt's bully pulpit.

The greatest presidents in the scholars' rankings, Washington, Lincoln, and Franklin Roosevelt, were leaders who confronted and overcame the republic's greatest crises. Crisis widens presidential opportunities for bold and imaginative action. But it does not guarantee presidential greatness. The crisis of secession did not spur Buchanan or the crisis of depression spur Hoover to creative leadership. Their inadequacies in the face of crisis allowed Lincoln and the second Roosevelt to show the difference individuals make to history. Still, even in the absence of first-order crisis, forceful and persuasive presidents—Jackson, Theodore Roosevelt, Ronald Reagan—are able to impose their own priorities on the country.

The diverse drama of the presidency offers a fascinating set of tales. Biographies of American presidents constitute a chronicle of wisdom and folly, nobility and pettiness, courage and cunning, forthrightness and deceit, quarrel and consensus. The turmoil perennially swirling around the White House illuminates the heart of the American democracy.

It is the aim of the American Presidents series to present the grand panorama of our chief executives in volumes compact enough for the busy reader, lucid enough for the student, authoritative enough for the scholar. Each volume offers a distillation of character and career. I hope that these lives will give readers some understanding of the pitfalls and potentialities of the presidency and also of the responsibilities of citizenship. Truman's famous sign—"The buck stops here"—tells only half the story. Citizens cannot escape the ultimate responsibility. It is in the voting booth, not on the presidential desk, that the buck finally stops.

—Arthur M. Schlesinger, Jr.

John Quincy Adams

1

A Privileged Young Man

Toward the end of the presidential campaign of 1824, John Quincy Adams, one of the four candidates for the office, left his duties as secretary of state in Washington and returned to his home in Quincy, Massachusetts, there to roam around the cemetery and look at tombstones of his ancestors and meditate on the past and future. He walked among the graves of the four generations of his father's family. He singled out the tomb of Henry Adams, the first to come from England and settle in Braintree, now Quincy, around 1640; then there was Joseph Adams, Sr., and his wife, Abigail Baxter, and Joseph Adams, Jr., and his second wife, Hannah Bass.

John Quincy Adams paused for a bit and gazed at the grave of his paternal grandfather, John Adams, Sr., and his wife, Susannah Boylston. The family continues to grow, he mused. Now, in 1824, there were three succeeding generations of male Adamses still living: his father, John Adams, the former president; himself, the present secretary of state, and his brother, Thomas Boylston; and then the third generation, among whom were his children: George Washington, John II, and Charles Francis. "Pass another century," Adams noted in his diary, "and we shall all be mouldering in the same dust." I wonder, he added, "who then of our posterity shall visit this yard? And what shall he read engraved upon the stones?"

Since then another century and more have passed and surely those who look upon the graves of this family cannot but recognize that here lie the remains of supremely gifted men and women who served their country with distinction and added to its luster.

The secretary did not mention his mother's ancestors in his musings—and that could be an important key in understanding his character and personality—but they too brought a degree of greatness to the family tree. He was named after his maternal great-grandfather, John Quincy, who "died on the 13th of July, 1767, the day after I had received his name in baptism," the secretary later wrote. His mother, Abigail Smith, the daughter of the Reverend William Smith and his wife, Elizabeth Quincy Smith, both descendants from distinguished Massachusetts clergymen, was a feisty woman of remarkable intelligence and determination, a woman of high moral standards who set goals for her offspring that they spent their lives trying to achieve.

It was especially difficult for John Quincy Adams. He was the oldest boy in the family, born July 11, 1767, but his sister Abigail, called "Nabby" by the family, had preceded him by two years. Another sister, Susanna, followed him but died the following year, in February 1770; then came Charles who arrived on May 29, 1770, and Thomas on September 15, 1772. Johnny, as the family called him, was perpetually lectured about how he was the oldest son and had to set an example for his siblings. He had been born with gifts few others enjoyed, they told him, and was expected to live up to them and become a "great man." Over and over, year after year, his parents reminded him that he was privileged by birth and education, that he was destined to be "a Guardian of the Laws, Liberty and Religion of your Country," and that he must achieve a distinction in this life that would add to the family's already illustrious record of accomplishment.

Abigail actually took Johnny to Bunker Hill on June 17, 1775, to witness the famous battle so that he could better understand the price of freedom and the trials necessary to gain and defend it. He was all of seven years of age. Years later he still remembered "Britannia's thunders . . . and witnessed the tears of my mother and mingled with them my own" over the death of "a dear friend of my father," Dr. Joseph Warren, who fell in the conflict. It seems unbelievable, but this young boy was made to stand and watch the killing of men he knew! It must have been traumatic. From that moment on Abigail "taught me to repeat daily, after the Lord's prayer, before rising from bed, the Ode of Collins on the patriot warriors who fell in the war to subdue the Jacobite rebellion of 1745."

What a terrible burden to lay on a child. And because his parents relentlessly spelled out his duties, reprimanded him when he failed to live up to them, and corrected every move he made that seemed to contradict their expectations of him, it is not surprising that he developed into a very introverted, self-critical individual of enormous pride and low personal esteem who suffered periodic and deep mental depressions. In later years he admitted that he was "a man of reserved, cold, austere and forbidding manners." He recognized that people saw him as "a gloomy misanthropist" and "a social savage," but, he added, "I have not the pliability to reform it."

He really yearned for the life of the mind. Literature, the arts, and science were what genuinely interested him. Instead the family decreed a life serving the law (which he hated) to be followed by public service, an essential component for the recognition expected of him. Although he had few political talents and refused throughout his life to do that which would actively advance his public career, still he loved the influence that came with high office. He loved the power by which he could advance the well-being of all the people, and he loved the accompanying acclaim that naturally flowed from it.

His parents also drilled into him the importance of religion in his life and the obligation of maintaining strict observance of Christian moral values. When he took his first long trip away from home at the age of ten, Abigail admonished him to "adhere to those religious sentiments and principles which were early instilled into your mind, and remember that you are accountable to your Maker for all your words and actions." She had seen her own brother succumb to alcohol and debauchery, desert his family, and leave them penniless. If it took every ounce of strength in her body, she meant to protect her children from a similar fate. "Your passions are strong and impetuous," she told her son, "and tho I have sometimes seen them hurry you to excesses, yet with pleasure I have observed . . . your Efforts to govern and subdue them." All his life he kept up a lively battle "to govern and subdue" his passions, but his efforts never fully satisfied him. Johnny's father, one of the first New England Unitarians, weighed in on the subject by reminding him that "Your Conscience is the Minister Plenipotentiary of God Almighty in your Breast. See to it, that this Minister never negotiates in vain. Attend to him, in Opposition to all the Courts in the World."

Like the dutiful son he remained through life, John Quincy Adams adhered to these admonitions and, as an adult, read the Bible each morning for an hour in English, French, or German. According to his lights, it was the proper way to start the day. He regretted not knowing Hebrew so he could enjoy the original. And on Sunday he invariably attended two and sometimes three church services of different denominations, depending on his evaluation of the minister's intellectual strengths and preaching ability. "There is scarcely a Sunday passes . . . ," he later wrote in his diary, "in attendance upon divine service, I hear something of which a pointed application to my own situation and circumstances occurs to my thoughts. It is often consolation, support, encouragement—sometimes warning and admonition, sometimes keen and trying remembrance of deep distress." Raised as an independent Congregationalist, he finally joined the Unitarian Church in Quincy upon his father's death in 1826.

Naturally Johnny's education received special attention, particularly since he was expected to rise to greatness. He never went to school in Quincy but was educated at home by tutors: James Thaxter, his cousin, and Nathan Rice, one of his father's law clerks. Of course his parents took a very active role in his education. His father regularly instructed Abigail on Johnny's training. Fix his "Attention upon great and glorious Objects, root out every little Thing, weed out every Meanness," make him "great and manly." John Adams urged his son to revere scholarship as his "preeminent entertainment." Latin and Greek constituted the basic foundation for any educated man in the eighteenth century, and Johnny diligently memorized their grammar and vocabularies. In addition his father advised him to read history so that he could be better equipped to recognize evil and treachery in the world; and by all means he must study Thucydides' *History of the Peloponnesian War* in the original, "the most perfect of all human Languages," he was told. At the age of seven he wrote his father and said, "I hope I grow a better Boy and that you will have no occasion to be ashamed of me. . . . Mr. Thaxter says I learn my Books well—he is a very good Master. I read my Books to Mamma."

Not surprisingly, considering his education at the hands of such God-fearing, New England Puritan descendants as Abigail and John Adams, their son developed a towering guilt complex and throughout his life readily admitted to his many failings. Even at an early age Johnny had begun berating himself for his inadequacies. "My Thoughts are running after birds eggs play and trifles, till I get vexed with my Self," he wrote at age ten. "Mamma has a troublesome task to keep me Steady, and I own I am ashamed of myself."

It is amazing that he did not rebel over the demands placed upon him. Whatever anger raged within him, if such did exist, remained under tight control, although at times he later showed marked disrespect to his mother when he failed to answer her letters despite her frequent demands for a response. Toward his father he never seems to have had anything but the greatest respect and reverence. After all, John Adams was an extremely successful Boston lawyer, a man of the highest integrity who turned to politics when the British government passed the Intolerable Acts in 1774, which, among other things, closed the port of Boston and the courts of law. Sucked into the revolutionary stirrings rapidly developing, John Adams hurried off to Philadelphia to attend the Continental Congress where he joined a committee with Thomas Jefferson and Benjamin Franklin to write a Declaration of Independence.

With the Revolution now in full swing the Congress appointed a diplomatic commission, consisting of Benjamin Franklin, Arthur Lee, and Silas Deane, to obtain European assistance for the country's struggle to gain its freedom from England. But when the Congress recalled Deane to answer charges of improper conduct at the French court, it replaced him with Adams.

Although crossing the Atlantic Ocean would be extremely dangerous because of the presence of British frigates patrolling the coastline, the family decided that young Johnny was of an age where he needed a father's "example and precepts" so that "the foundations of a great man" could be laid. Besides, the experience abroad would be invaluable in shaping his future career. As for Abigail and the other children, they would remain at home.

So in February 1778 the new commissioner and his son boarded the frigate *Boston* and headed into a stormy ocean. Despite a harrowing crossing, they arrived safely in Bordeaux on April 1. Seven days later they reached Paris where Benjamin Franklin, already in residence, invited them to stay at his home in Passy, a suburb near the Bois de Boulogne. Johnny entered a private boarding school at Passy run by Monsieur Le Coeur where he studied French, Latin, and mathematics, along with fencing, dancing, and drawing. Several other American boys attended the school, including William Templeton Franklin and Benjamin Franklin Bache, the grandsons of Benjamin Franklin. Classes began at 6 in the morning and continued for two hours, after which they were given a sixty-minute respite for breakfast and play. Then there were classes from 9 to noon, 2 to 4:30 P.M., and 5 to 7:30. In between times the students were allowed recreation and meals. They retired at 9 P.M.

Although thousands of miles away, Abigail reached across the ocean to remind her son never to "disgrace his mother" and be "worthy of his father." "Dear as you are to me," she wrote, "I had much rather you should have found your Grave in the ocean you have crossed, or any untimely death crop you in your Infant years, rather than see you an immoral profligate or a Graceless child." Just remember, "you must keep a strict guard upon yourself, or the odious monster will soon loose its terror by becoming familiar to you."

She never let up. But she need not have concerned herself. Always conscious of his moral duties, Johnny also proved to be a diligent scholar and demonstrated remarkable progress in his studies. He mastered the French language quite rapidly, much to his father's delight, and the talent served him well for the remainder of his life.

Johnny learned to love something else in France: theater. It was an enthusiasm that provided him with lifelong pleasure. He also enjoyed concerts and opera and soon developed a taste for the music of Bellini and Rossini.

Unfortunately the two Adamses did not remain long in Europe. When they arrived, John Adams found that the other commissioners had already signed treaties of commerce and alliance with France on February 6, 1778. As a consequence Congress recalled him, and he and his son left Paris on March 8, 1779, and boarded the French frigate *Sensible*, which set sail for America on June 17. Accompanying them aboard the ship was the Chevalier de la Luzerne, France's first envoy to the United States, and his secretary, Barbé Marbois. During the voyage Johnny tutored the two Frenchmen in the English language and they found him an absolute delight. As John Adams recorded in his diary, they "are in raptures with my son. . . . The Ambassador said he was astonished at my son's knowledge; that he was a master of his own language, like a professor."

Father and son arrived back in Boston on August 2. But they had hardly unpacked their belongings and settled down to the routine of daily life at home when Congress ordered Adams to return to Europe. Spain had offered to assist in arbitrating a peace treaty between England and France, and Congress wanted Adams present to make certain the negotiations guaranteed American independence. Congress appointed him minister plenipotentiary.

This time the new minister did not intend to take Johnny with him to Paris, and his son was just as pleased to remain home. The lad wished to attend Andover Academy to prepare for admission to Harvard, just as the family had decided. But Abigail had other ideas. She flatly informed Johnny that another tour in France would awaken in his mind "the character of the hero and the statesman." In all "human probability," she added, "it will do more for your education to go back to France with your father than to prepare for college at Andover." Besides, he was incapable "of judgeing what was most for your own benefit." In addition, Johnny's younger brother, Charles, would accompany him, along with Francis Dana, the secretary of the peace commission, and John Thaxter, private secretary to the minister, who would also act as tutor. It would make for a splendid balance of family and friends who would watch over the boys and teach and guide them. The opportunities were too obvious and valuable to be lost.

He must go, she announced, and that ended the discussion. Just make certain "that your improvements . . . bear some proportion to your advantages," she lectured Johnny. "Nothing is wanting with you, but attention, dilligence and steady application. Nature has not been deficient."

Dutifully Johnny agreed, and, as required, asked his father for permission to accompany him. John Adams readily consented and urged his son to keep a diary so that he could record all the important events he would experience and people he would meet in Europe. The exercise would also help improve his penmanship, something his father insisted upon. "My Pappa enjoins upon me to keep a journal, or diary of the Events that happen to me, and of objects that I See, and of Characters that I converse with from day to day, and altho I am Convinced of the utility, importance & necessity of this Exercise, yet I have not patience and perseverance enough to do it so Constantly as I ought."

True, Johnny was at first very haphazard about keeping this journal and six months passed before he actually made an entry. But with the passage of several years he became more addicted to it and sometimes spent six hours a day recording not only his thoughts and ideas but who he had seen or spoken with, where he went, what he read, who he liked and (mainly) disliked, what he ate and drank, what churches he attended, what historic places he visited, the merit of the sermons he heard, what the weather was like, and on and on. The complete diary is an absolute treasure trove of information about the early nineteenth century. John Quincy's son, Charles Francis Adams, edited and published this enormous manuscript in twelve volumes, omitting certain parts that he deemed personal and private. Later, nineteen reels of microfilm were necessary to contain this gargantuan record. No work of history about the antebellum period of U.S. history can afford to neglect it. It is one of the many blessings John Quincy Adams left to posterity.

"My Pappa, who takes a great deal of Pains to put me in the right way," he continued, "has also advised me to Preserve Copies of all my letters, & has given me a Convenient Blank Book for this end." He naturally felt himself unequal to the task and feared that in the future when he looked back on "my Childish nonsense," he would be ashamed and disgusted; still he hoped it would demonstrate how he had "advanced, in taste, judgment, & knowledge." Later in life he said that "a letter-book, a diary, a book of receipts and expenses— these three books, kept without intermission, should be the rule of duty of every man who can read and write." It requires, he went on, perseverance and "a character to which toil is a pleasure, and of which untiring patience is an essential element."

The first entry of the diary appeared on Friday, November 12, 1779, the day before Johnny began his second trip to Europe, aboard the French frigate *Sensible,* and the voyage proved as dangerous and frightening as the first. This was the same ship that had brought him and his father home, and it endured so many storms during this return that the hull cracked and the captain was forced to head for the nearest port. They landed in Ferrol at the northwestern tip of Spain on December 18, 1779, and it took a week before they could gather their gear and head for Paris. After a particularly slow and rough journey over treacherous mountains they reached Paris on February 9 and took quarters at the Hotel de Valois. Once settled the boys resumed their education at the local academy.

Poor Charles was absolutely miserable. At nine years of age he had trouble adapting to a European culture. He was homesick and it grew steadily worse over the next year. Still he struggled to keep going. After all it was expected of him. As an Adams he could never admit defeat—how could he face his mother? But he wept uncontrollably. The effect on his general well-being must have been devastating. By the following year his several illnesses and continued longing for home finally convinced his father to send him back to Braintree.

As expected Abigail remained a real presence to her sons despite the thousands of miles that separated them. She constantly warned Johnny about the temptations and allurements of Europe and begged him to show strength in warding them off. "If you could once feel how grateful to the heart of a parent the good conduct of a child is, you would never be the occasion of exciting any other sensation in the bosom of your ever affectionate mother." Above all, "let your ambition be engaged to become eminent." You have a duty to yourself, your family, and your country—and she pounded out this message without pause.

Johnny rewarded her constant harassment with silence. When she complained about his failure to respond to her letters ("I have suffered great anxiety in not hearing from . . . you," she wrote him), he reminded her that he was spending all his time with his studies as he knew she wished him to do.

The rapid progress he made at the academy amazed his father. John Adams had to admit that his son "learned more French in a day than I could learn in a Week with all my books." All of which was conveyed to the ever-watchful, ever-fearful, ever-nagging Abigail.

Johnny's education was switched to Holland when his father decided that the French were uncooperative in seeking a termination of the war and that he would be better off moving to Amsterdam where he hoped to persuade the Dutch to provide financial aid to the struggling American nation. So the boys were plucked out of the academy and on July 27, 1780, the commissioner and his sons headed for the Netherlands. Once they arrived in Amsterdam Johnny and Charles were enrolled in the Latin School to continue their studies. But they hated it. The rector abused and humiliated them, which Johnny dutifully reported to his father. The senior Adams withdrew his children and then decided that they were mature enough to attend the renowned University of Leyden. There they would study under the direction of a family friend, Benjamin Waterhouse, who was presently working toward a medical degree.

Johnny loved the place. Virtually an independent scholar, he reveled in the intellectual excitement he found in attending lectures, and he enjoyed the private tutoring he received. Again demonstrating remarkable aptitude, he was formally admitted by the institution as a university scholar in January 1781. His father instructed him to attend "all the Lectures in which Experiments are made whether in Philosophy, Medicine or Chimistry [sic], because they will open your mind for Inquiries into Nature; but by no means neglect the Languages." But Abigail had reservations about this Holland adventure. At least, she advised Johnny, try to emulate the "universal neatness and Cleanliness" for which the Dutch are noted. Hopefully it "will cure you of all your slovenly tricks, and that you will learn from them industry, oconomy [sic] and frugality."

In the midst of this idyllic life Congress decided to seek the support of the Russian government and dispatched Francis Dana to St. Petersburg in the hope that he could induce Catherine the Great to recognize American independence. Spain, the ally of France, had recently declared war against Great Britain, after which Catherine warned that the Russian navy would protect her nation's trade against all belligerents, an action that threatened British blockade efforts against France and Spain. Then, in early July 1780, she invited other European nations to join a League of Armed Neutrality for their mutual protection, an invitation that was quickly snapped up by Denmark and Sweden, followed by the Netherlands, Prussia, Portugal, Austria, and the Kingdom of the Two Sicilies. This action prompted Congress to appoint Dana as minister to Russia with the expectation that he would gain entry to the league through a formal treaty with Russia that could lead to recognition of American independence by all the other European countries.

But Dana faced a real problem. He had little knowledge of French, the language spoken at the Russian court. He therefore needed someone who knew French well enough to interpret, translate, and copy official messages. At that point John Adams offered Johnny. Only fourteen years old at the time, the young man was quite mature for his age and very skilled in the French language. Besides, he had shown a remarkable capacity for concentrated work. To serve in this position, meet important people at court, and observe events reshaping the world would be of incalculable value for the boy. Dana was delighted with the suggestion and on July 7, 1781, the new American diplomatic team headed east toward St. Petersburg, a distance of twenty-four hundred miles.

Their first major stop was Berlin, the capital of the Kingdom of Prussia, which Johnny thought was "a very pretty town, much more so than Paris." But when he arrived in St. Petersburg on August 27, he was completely charmed with its beauty and pronounced it his favorite. But that was the extent of his admiration. It quickly developed that Catherine had no intention of obliging America's expectations. As a result the social life of Dana and Johnny was severely limited; worse, the young student could not find a school where he could continue his studies. "There is nobody here but Princes and

Slaves," he wrote his father. "The Slaves cannot have their children instructed, and the nobility that chuse to have their's send them into foreign countries. There is not one school to be found in the whole city." So Johnny undertook his own education. He found an English library in the city and read Cicero, Voltaire, Pope, Addison, Dryden, Hume, Macaulay, commenced the study of German, perfected his French, and practiced his Latin and Greek. He also began what became a lifelong habit of browsing bookstores, buying what he thought valuable and interesting and sending them home to start his own private library. Of course he found the Russian winter a horror. There was very little to interest him in the capital and he started feeling guilty about wasting his time, which could be better spent at home at an academy preparing for admission to Harvard.

But in some ways the long fourteen months he spent on his own, away from direct parental control, were unbelievably liberating. The only restraints on him were those that he himself imposed. In her letters Abigail naturally continued to browbeat him about dressing properly and remaining pure and undefiled in the midst of European sin and temptation but he simply ignored her. Months passed without a single letter to his mother, which naturally resulted in even more stinging rebukes. In one letter she charged him with forgetting her. "Has the cold Northern Regions . . . chilled your affections, or obliterated the Remembrance of her who gave you Birth?" Have I been "forgotten by my Son?"

That brought a response. He swore that "my reverence for the dearest and most honoured of mothers" had not waned in the slightest. In fact it had grown during his absence from her. He said he "scratch'd out of your letter these words, *to be forgotten by my Son*, for I could not bear to think that such an Idea should ever have entered the mind of my ever honoured Mamma." The problem, he protested, was the unreliability of the Russian mail and the difficulty of getting letters through to the West.

Abigail accepted his excuses "but you must give them further energy by a steady attention to your pen in future," she lectured. After "two years silence . . . you cannot know . . . the feelings of a parent. . . . What is it that affectionate parents require of their

Children; for all their care, anxiety and toil on their accounts? Only that they would be wise and virtuous, Benevolent and kind."

Johnny's father had also become concerned by his silence. He repeatedly warned his son about the dangers of the corrupt Russian court where "innocence and a pure conscience" were constantly on trial. Both Abigail and John Adams never wrote their son without instructing, criticizing, berating, warning, or admonishing him—all for his own good of course. Their rules and advice for leading a virtuous life alone would fill a modest-size book.

Finally, his concern mounting each day, his father summoned Johnny back to The Hague. All things considered, he said—the unavailability of formal schooling, the fact that the mission was stillborn since the Americans were virtually ignored in the capital, and the dangers of St. Petersburg to the morals of a teenage boy—convinced him that his son should leave Russia and either return to his studies at the University of Leyden or serve as his private secretary in place of John Thaxter, who was going home.

With a second Russian winter close at hand, Johnny was delighted to vacate St. Petersburg. As soon as the necessary departure permission was obtained he left for Stockholm on October 30, 1782, and arrived on November 22. So hospitable and friendly were the Swedes, so many friends did he make in a brief period of time, so many parties and masquerades did he attend within days of his arrival, so many exhilarating and informative conversations did he have that he decided to extend his stay in the country for several weeks.

It was another liberating experience. It marked the beginning of a new phase in his life, one in which he grew enormously, both socially and intellectually. At the age of fifteen he had matured into an adult. He suddenly realized that he had full control of his life, and he reveled in it. He had become his own man and he expected to be treated like an adult, not as a child who needed constant supervision and lecturing about his morals and dress. At the many dinners, parties, and balls he attended in the Swedish capital he exuded a charm and gaiety that the Swedes found captivating in one so young. They genuinely liked this intelligent, articulate, and handsome young man, and he liked them. "I believe there is no people in Europe so civil and hospitable to Strangers as the Sweeds." He hated to leave such a congenial place and so he stayed until mid-February, enjoying the luxury of a short but stimulating period of liberation.

While Johnny was living a life relatively free of parental constraints, John Adams had been working diligently to win Dutch assistance. Finally, on March 28, 1782, the Province of Holland recognized American independence, and on April 19 the States-General of the Dutch Republic acknowledged Adams as ambassador of the United States. The delighted envoy hung out a flag at what he called the Hotel des Etats Unis, the first American embassy in Europe.

Two months later he scored a second triumph. He negotiated a loan of $2 million at 5 percent interest with three banking houses in Amsterdam. More than anything else the loan helped establish American credit in Europe, although the loan was smaller than he anticipated. Then, on October 8, he signed a treaty of commerce with the Dutch Republic, completing a notable string of diplomatic successes. All that now remained was working out a formal treaty of peace with Great Britain.

Congress notified Adams that he would no longer serve as the sole deputy in the peace negotiations in Paris. A commission had been set up that would include (besides Adams) Benjamin Franklin, John Jay, Henry Laurens, who arrived late, and Thomas Jefferson, who did not serve. Meanwhile, on October 18, 1781, Lord Cornwallis had surrendered his army to General Washington at Yorktown. The war for independence, for all intents and purposes, was ended.

John Quincy finally left Stockholm on January 1, 1783, and stopped off for a month at the port city of Göteborg where the French consul provided introductions that allowed him to meet important people and attend parties and a masquerade ball. Rather reluctantly he left Göteborg on February 11, crossed into Denmark, then slowly made his way to Hamburg, stayed a month, and finally reached The Hague on April 21, when he notified his father, who had gone to Paris, of his arrival.

It was a different, more mature John Quincy Adams who returned to the Netherlands. Although not yet sixteen, he had become something of a celebrity among the socially elite. He was a skilled linguist, a classicist of sorts, a superb conversationalist whose knowledge of literature, the arts, and science set him apart. Moreover, he was American, a rather unique distinction in social circles at that time.

Interestingly, he resumed writing his diary after a long hiatus, a work that now reflected his maturity in detailing what he saw and experienced and felt.

A very relieved, if rather annoyed, parent hurried back to The Hague to greet his son whom he had not seen in two years. And when they met on July 22, John Adams was flabbergasted by the appearance and presence of his son. This was no child, no boy. "He is grown a Man in Understanding as well as Stature," John Adams reported to his wife. At sixteen JQA, which is how he frequently referred to himself, stood five feet seven inches tall. Moderately handsome with a stocky build, he startlingly resembled his father, receding hairline and all. The two men quickly became friends in the way they treated and spoke to one another, and when the father informed his son that he could resume his studies at the University of Leyden or tutor with him and serve as his private secretary, the young man unhesitatingly chose the latter option.

Abigail took exception to her son's indifference to her anxiety and "ordered" (JQA's word) him to give her his "observations on the countries" he had visited. In a snide aside she remarked that she did not expect either "precisian [sic]" or "elegance" in his descriptions but she did want to know what he had done and seen.

The trouble with Abigail, according to Adams's most recent biographer, Paul Nagel, is that she needed to dominate her children. She could not let go. As such, he concludes, she was "a calamity as a mother." Indeed.

In August 1783 father and son returned to Paris where John Adams resumed negotiations to end the war. Since France was suspected of looking out for its own interest, the three commissioners decided to disobey their instructions about consulting the French on any peace proposal and proceed on their own initiative. After considerable discussion they signed the final peace treaty ending the war on September 3, 1783; the treaty recognized U.S. independence and set a western boundary at the Mississippi River. In addition, thanks to the efforts of John Adams, the new nation retained the right to fish off British North America and cure the catch on unsettled shores in Labrador, the Magdalen Islands, and Nova Scotia. The French, although surprised and shocked by the behavior of their ally, were anxious to end the war with England and accepted Franklin's tactful explanation for the actions of the commissioners.

John Quincy assisted in the preparation of the papers involved in drawing up the treaty and attended all the functions and events to which his father was invited, especially the parties and receptions. He proved to be an invaluable aide and secretary, and his father introduced him to the "foreign Ministers, and all the Principal People." He became well acquainted with diplomatic documents and language, and intimate with Benjamin Franklin and Thomas Jefferson after the latter's arrival in Paris. He spent many days and evenings with Jefferson, talking about literature, science, the arts, history, and government. His diary frequently mentioned that he "dined at Mr. Jefferson's" or "spent the evening with Mr. Jefferson, whom I love to be with." Without question, he added, "Mr. Jefferson is a man of universal learning." For his part Jefferson took great interest in Johnny, so much so that the father later told the Virginian that "he appeared to me as much your boy as mine."

When Congress decided that John Adams would remain in Europe on various assignments, the envoy urged his wife and daughter to join him. It had been four years since his departure from America, an absence that had taken a heavy toll on the family. "Who shall compensate to me those *years* I cannot recall?" Abigail complained. "How dearly have I paid for a titled husband."

So she and Nabby sailed for England on June 20, 1784, and arrived a month later. Because of the press of business John Adams could not meet his family and therefore sent his son to greet them. When the seventeen-year-old man entered his mother's hotel room in London she scarcely recognized him. It was quite a shock. He looked much older than she expected and now closely resembled his father in appearance. Here stood a European gentleman, indeed a very imposing gentleman, and Abigail was not sure she quite approved the change. Nabby pronounced him a "sober lad" but one she expected to get to know better in the months ahead. A week later John Adams appeared and after a joyful reunion led his family back to Paris where he, Franklin, and Jefferson were to negotiate treaties of amity and commerce with various European powers.

In Paris John Quincy had the pleasure of guiding his mother and sister around the city, pointing out historic monuments and important buildings. They attended art galleries, the opera, concerts, and theater. The family rented a house in Auteuil where they remained for the next nine months until John Adams was officially notified on April 26, 1785, that he had been appointed minister to the Court of St. James, while Jefferson was to replace Franklin as minister to France.

For John Quincy Adams it was time to make an important decision in his life: either remain in Europe and continue to luxuriate in the culture of a highly sophisticated society or return home to complete his formal education and find a career for himself. The family discussed the matter at length and agreed that he should return and attend Harvard College. Abigail was particularly insistent that he give up the pleasures of Europe for the practical life that he would find in America. But it was John Quincy himself who recognized where his future lay. He said he had seen his father give a lifetime of service to the interests of the country and had little to show for it. "His own fortune has suffered by it." As a result Adams's children must provide for themselves, "which I shall never be able to do, if I loiter away my precious time in Europe." In America "I can live *independent and free*," he exclaimed with heightened enthusiasm, and he was determined "not to fall into the same error" as his father.

So he arranged to sail home. He left Europe on May 21 and on July 17, 1785, arrived back in New York City, at that time the nation's capital where a new government had been established under the Articles of Confederation. In his diary John Quincy could not help wondering about the merit of giving up the intellectual splendors of the ancient University of Leyden for a small school like Harvard. Still he knew there was no future for him in Europe.

Many years later at the age of forty-two he came to regret the time he had spent abroad because, he said, it stunted his education. His studies had been all so haphazard and informal; they lacked organization and purpose. And the almost two-year interval in Russia was a complete waste of time. "Hence it has happened," he wrote, "that, though I was always of a studious turn and addicted to books beyond bounds of moderation, yet my acquirements in literature and science have been all superficial, and I never attained a profound knowledge of anything."

How wrong he was. What he failed to appreciate were the things he had actually gained. Here at the age of eighteen he was a fiercely intelligent and independent young man about to enter Harvard, mature beyond his years, broadly read in history and literature, conversant on a wide range of subjects, fluent in French, and extraordinarily knowledgeable about European court life and society, having traveled across much of Europe and talked with all classes of citizens. He had also benefited from the wisdom and experience of Thomas Jefferson, Benjamin Franklin, Francis Dana, and others, visited many historical sites, and gained an appreciation of music and theater that provided him with a lifetime of pleasure. It was an incomparable education, one that better prepared him for his future career as diplomat and statesman than any training he might have received at home. He was indeed a very privileged young man.

2

Finding a Career

Beginning study at Harvard proved more troublesome than anyone might have imagined for someone with the pedigree and background of John Quincy Adams. But President Joseph Willard chose to query the young man and found him sadly deficient in Latin and Greek. He therefore advised him to spend the next fall and winter studying these subjects privately so that he could be admitted. In view of his record of study abroad, if he successfully passed another examination at the end of that time he would be permitted to enter junior year in April 1786 for the remaining three months of the term.

Shocked, humiliated, and deeply disappointed, John Quincy accepted this blow, no doubt justifying it as a corrective to his overweening pride. He spent the next several months at the home of his uncle, the Reverend Joseph Shaw, Abigail's brother-in-law, where he studied to repair his educational deficiencies, and in the spring he was duly admitted to Harvard as a junior. His parents were naturally delighted that "our dear old Alma Mater," as his father put it, had accepted Johnny, and the young man was warned against doing anything that might be remembered later with "shame or pain."

For the next fifteen months John Quincy enjoyed his program of studies at Harvard, particularly science and mathematics. And, like Frederick the Great, he took up the flute in an effort to learn more about the science of music so as to increase his enjoyment of it. He was admitted to Phi Beta Kappa, and in one of his addresses before the society argued that fortune rather than love should be the chief inducement to marriage. He dismissed passion since it was so transitory and insisted that a successful marriage had to be based on reason. He graduated second out of a class of fifty-one, and in his commencement address—one of four so chosen—he stirringly invoked the need for patriotic self-sacrifice, the same that had characterized those who fought and won the Revolution. And he strongly maintained the necessity of restoring the financial health of the nation so that its integrity and honor would be acknowledged abroad and perpetuated forever. It was all very extravagant and bedecked with literary and classical allusions but it was perfect for the occasion.

There hardly seemed to be any doubt what profession John Quincy would pursue upon graduation in 1787, even though he had little interest and less aptitude for the law. But that is what his parents and everyone else seemed to expect of him and he followed right along without a murmur of dissent. So, three months later, in September, he entered the Newburyport office of Theophilus Parsons and began the study of law along with four other students. Parsons was a celebrated New England attorney who would later serve as chief justice of the Massachusetts Supreme Court.

During the next several years, while John Quincy slaved over Blackstone and Coke, the thirteen states set aside the Articles of Confederation and adopted a new Constitution by which George Washington was elected president of the United States and John Adams, who had returned from England, was chosen vice president. The nation had emerged from difficult times under the Articles, and only through the formation of this new Union did the country begin to establish itself as a successful experiment in freedom and republican government.

John Quincy also fell deeply in love with a beautiful young sixteen-year-old by the name of Mary Frazier, the daughter of Moses Frazier, a prominent citizen in Newburyport. After a few months the romance quickly developed into a serious relationship. John and Mary took long walks together and felt boundless joy in one another's company. When possible they attended parties and the theater together, and he wrote poetry about her and to her. Quite obviously the young man's emotions had carried him to the point of asking for Mary's hand in marriage, but reason kept reminding him that he could not support a wife. He was twenty-three years of age and still dependent on his parents' support; and although his apprenticeship in the law was coming to an end, it would take time to establish a practice and earn enough money to afford a wife. Besides, his parents insisted he open his law office in Boston, not Newburyport, which he preferred because of Mary's presence.

Dutifully he removed to Boston when his law studies ended, and on July 15, 1790, was duly sworn into practice. Three weeks later he opened his law office in a house owned by his father on Court Street. But few clients came. His courtship of Mary continued as best he could manage it and there seemed to be every indication that he planned to marry her. Unfortunately Abigail learned of the romance and immediately intervened. She notified her son that she was stunned and incredulous when she learned "that you are attached to a young lady." "Never form connections until you see a prospect of supporting a wife," she lectured in a series of letters. An early marriage "will involve you in troubles that may render you and yours unhappiness for the remainder of your life."

The son chose to disregard his mother's warning and advice. He asked his beloved to agree to acknowledge their love and pledge to marry as soon as he could establish himself and support a family. But Mary's family would not accept such an "indefinite" arrangement and insisted on a formal engagement, something John Quincy could not and would not do. Mary came to Boston to discuss it with him—and she held her ground. There must be an agreement such as her family demanded, she informed him, or they must end their relationship.

Totally dependent upon his family, John felt powerless to disobey them and with "broken heart" he terminated their romance. Shortly thereafter he informed Abigail that she need worry no longer. "I am perfectly free, and you may rest assured I shall remain so. . . . I may add I was never in less danger from any entanglement which can give you pain than at present."

As far as can be judged, this was the only romantic and passionate love of John Quincy Adams's entire life. It took a long time before he ceased to grieve over his lost love. Nearly fifty years later he admitted that Mary was "to me the most beautiful and most beloved of her sex." They had pledged themselves to each other, he said. "Dearly! how dearly did the sacrifice of her cost me, voluntary as it was" since she insisted "upon a positive engagement or a separation." Four long years "of exquisite wretchedness followed" and the "wound in my bosom" did not heal "till the Atlantic Ocean flowed between us."

Small wonder his law practice did not take hold. To add to his misery he lost his first case in court. These failures triggered the return of a recurring depression that plagued him much of his life. Such despair could paralyze his mental and physical activities and leave him wallowing in self-pity and self-reproach. He survived these trying days of 1790 by immersing himself in literature, science, the theater, and music. He had always enjoyed writing and had had some limited success. In an effort to free himself from his heartache he turned to it again and published a series of essays in 1791 entitled "Letters of Publicola" in the Boston *Columbian Centinel*. These eleven essays were a reply to Thomas Paine's *The Rights of Man* in which Paine had called on the British people to imitate the French and overthrow the monarchy. Paine implied that the popular will suffered no limitations in what it could do to alter their government. In response Adams warned against demagoguery and insisted on protection of individual rights. In America, he said, those rights are protected under a constitutional system that had established a republican frame of government. God forbid that they could be endangered by a rampaging democracy intent on leveling existing distinctions in society by supposing it had the power and therefore the right to do whatever it wished.

These highly conservative views brought immediate approval by those who politically called themselves Federalists and favored the ideas espoused by Alexander Hamilton, the secretary of the treasury in the Washington administration. These ideas included support for a strong central government, payment of national and state debts by the central government, and the establishment of a national bank. Those who favored the rights of the states and worried over the possible despotism of a strong central government rallied around Thomas Jefferson, the secretary of state, and called themselves

Republicans. Individual rights could best be protected by the states, argued Jefferson, and he, like other Republicans, strongly opposed the creation of a central bank such as Hamilton had proposed.

Young Adams had clearly identified himself as a Federalist and with the publication of each succeeding essay he became something of a celebrity in Boston, particularly among the conservative upper classes. But Republicans denounced the "Letters" as a defense of aristocracy, elitism, and the British monarchical system as well as an attack on the French revolutionary forces that had overthrown hereditary privilege and monarchy.

The writing of these essays helped Adams deal with his broken heart and unsuccessful law practice and encouraged him to become politically active. He started by attending town meetings and serving as a committee member to improve security in Boston. He also responded to a request from Braintree citizens to help draft legislation to change the parish into a full-fledged town to be renamed Quincy after his great-grandfather, John Quincy. His success in this assignment brought him a small degree of pleasure and a heightened sense of accomplishment.

He was further prodded into the political arena when war broke out between Britain and France and President George Washington issued a proclamation of neutrality. The French minister to the United States, Edmond Genêt, attacked the president for his action, accused him of exceeding his powers, and urged Americans to privateer against the British. Washington responded by demanding Genêt's recall. Jefferson and his Republican allies generally had supported the minister and were reluctant to see him recalled.

At this point young Adams stepped in with another series of essays written under the names "Marcellus," "Columbus," and "Barneveld" that the *Columbian Centinel* and the Boston *Chronicle* published starting in the spring of 1793 and ending in January 1794. In these works, which were widely circulated, he not only defended Washington's actions but demonstrated a mastery of international law. He argued that privateering such as Genêt had recommended constituted "highway robbery" and should be dealt with as such. The United States, he concluded, must shun any effort to involve itself in European politics and wars.

The success of this defense brought him an invitation to deliver the Fourth of July oration in Boston, a unique honor and one he fulfilled with great distinction, predicting that the success of liberty in the United States would inspire the oppressed of the world to follow its example. An even greater honor followed in May 1794 when President Washington, no doubt at the behest of the vice president operating through the secretary of state, chose him to become the nation's minister resident in the Netherlands. Washington had noticed John Quincy's defense and was not only grateful for it but believed that it helped turn the tide of popular sentiment against Genêt and in favor of his recall.

Adams's parents were elated with the appointment since it meant that their son would now enter public service like his father and continue the tradition of bringing additional fame to the family. And nothing less than total success was expected of him. "If you do not rise to the head not only of your profession, but of your country," his father ranted at him, "it will be owing to your own *Laziness, Slovenliness,* and *Obstinacy.*" John Adams had obviously taken a page from Abigail's treatise on parent-child psychology.

John Quincy had no desire to leave the country now that his career had started to show some promise. Why was he not consulted about the appointment, he asked. "I rather wish it had not been made at all," he told his father. He also worried that it would be seen as nepotism, and the thought of leaving behind all his friends and family was "very painful." His youthfulness for such an important position—he was twenty-seven—also gave him pause. Still, it was a steady job that paid $4,500 a year and would free him from his financial dependence on his father.

His parents dismissed his objections and assured him that it was in his own best interests and that of his country. He had no choice, they said, but to accept. Furthermore, the United States had only five missions abroad—France, England, Spain, Portugal, and the Netherlands—and for John Quincy to be appointed to one of them and become the equal of James Monroe, Thomas Pinckney, William Short, and David Humphreys, the ministers in those respective countries, was a singular honor that must not be refused.

So in late June 1794 young Adams set out for Philadelphia, the then capital, to meet with the secretary of state, Edmund Randolph, and discuss the assignment and what was expected of him. He studied various documents as background and met and dined with other members of the cabinet and the administration. During this time in Philadelphia he also talked with his brother, Thomas Boylston Adams, and succeeded in convincing Tom to accompany him to the Netherlands as his secretary. Abigail and John instantly approved since young Tom was also having difficulty starting a legal career. At first Tom was reluctant to accept but when he was assured that the tour of duty would last no more than three years he consented.

The two brothers departed Boston on September 17, 1794, and after another stormy trip across the Atlantic docked in England on October 15 and reached London the following day. The reason for the stopover in London was to deliver papers to John Jay, chief justice of the United States, whom Washington had sent to England on a special mission to negotiate a trade treaty and settle other problems between the two countries, such as the impressment of American seamen and the seizure of U.S. ships. Unfortunately, the Jay Treaty, as finally written, was a disaster for the United States. It favored the British regarding trade and failed to resolve any of the other problems besetting the two nations. To Republicans it was a disgrace and a humiliation. But Washington realized it could prevent war between the two countries in these perilous times. He therefore accepted and submitted the treaty to the Senate where it was ratified on June 24, 1795.

For the next two weeks after their arrival in London the brothers enjoyed an active round of theater and party-going. Meanwhile, John Quincy waited for expected funds from the State Department that did not arrive in time so he was obliged to borrow money from Jay to finance his trip to Holland. He and his brother left London on October 28, crossed the Channel—another wrenching experience— and hurried on to The Hague where he immediately established his ministry. The French had already declared war against Holland and in January 1795 invaded the Netherlands. But John Quincy's fluency in French and his enjoyment of French company spared him the necessity of quitting his post during the invasion. He made The Hague a listening post by which he kept his government informed of important European developments as they occurred.

For the most part Adams had few diplomatic problems to address during his tenure but he did advise his government about the mounting success of French arms on the continent and the continuing necessity of maintaining strict neutrality. One by one, France toppled England's allies: the Netherlands, Prussia, and Spain in 1795 with Austria following soon after. All of which could lead to the closing of the continent to British trade and to any neutral nation, like the United States, who might try to do business with both sides.

President Washington was so impressed with Adams's ability as a diplomat that after signing the Jay Treaty he dispatched the young man to London to arrange for the exchange of ratifications. Jay had long since returned to America, and the U.S. minister to England, Thomas Pinckney, had gone to Spain. But by the time Adams arrived in London on November 11, 1795, the exchange of ratifications had already taken place with the legation secretary acting on his behalf.

Always delighted with London society John Quincy remained in England to represent his country until Pinckney's return from Spain in January 1796. During this interim he enjoyed not only the theater, the book stalls, and long walks with friends and acquaintances but the hospitality and company of the American consul, Joshua Johnson, his wife, and seven charming daughters, three of whom were of marriageable age.

Born in Maryland, Johnson had come to England prior to the Revolution as a factor for an Annapolis tobacco firm and married an Englishwoman, Catherine Nuth. During the Revolution he moved to France but returned to London as consul when the war ended. In addition to his salary as consul he seemed to have a thriving trading business, and his lifestyle reflected his apparent prosperity.

John Quincy took great pleasure in dining with Johnson and his family and in enjoying the entertainments provided by the several daughters who played and sang for him. He particularly liked dancing with the second daughter, Louisa. They soon became attached to each other and he seemed quite smitten. She had many outstanding attributes: beauty, intelligence, musical interest and ability, and knowledge of French, which she had learned while living in France with her family. Most particularly she behaved like a mature, self-confident woman, not flighty and silly like so many other girls he had met in America. But she also had an independent and assertive streak that sometimes disturbed him.

The romance, if it could be called such, continued through the winter and spring of 1796 with everyone wondering where it might lead. John Quincy was obviously quite taken with Louisa. But did he love her—enough to ask for her hand in marriage? Most probably he was content to allow the arrangement to simply drift along without a commitment on either side. But Mrs. Johnson had other ideas and demanded to know his intentions. Caught off guard, he admitted a desire to marry Louisa, which apparently satisfied the woman. After all, in many respects, Louisa was ideal, and not incidentally the exact opposite of Abigail. What better reason to marry the girl! He subsequently proposed to her and she accepted. But she showed her intense annoyance at him for not informing her first of his intentions.

It is most probable that at this point in his life John Quincy did not love Louisa—not the way he had loved Mary Frazier. His feelings lacked passion. But he was of an age when men were expected to marry. After all he had established himself, had a steady income, and could financially afford to take this momentous step. Moreover, the family seemed well off, which was an advantage (what better example of "reason and judgment" over transitory passion), and he certainly enjoyed her company. But did he really wish to marry or had he allowed himself to be maneuvered into making a commitment?

His uncertainty showed in his hesitation to set a wedding date. Repeatedly he fended off Louisa's insistence that he fulfill his promise to her. His own family also tried to deter him. Abigail fretted over the fact that Louisa was British. "I would hope for the love I bear my country," she wrote her son, "that the Siren is at least *half-blood*." Then it developed that there would be no dowry. The presumed wealth of Joshua Johnson suddenly disappeared. Due to a lifestyle beyond his means, mounting debts, bad investments, and perhaps mismanagement by agents and advisers, Johnson now faced financial ruin. When John Quincy learned of this misfortune he began to worry that his salary as minister resident would not be enough to support a family, especially a wife accustomed to a life of luxury.

So the betrothed departed for the Netherlands on May 28 without agreeing to a wedding date. Once back in harness at The Hague with his books, letter writing, reading, and light diplomatic duties, he felt a sense of relief. It was a comfortable life, he mused, one infinitely better suited to his personal taste, a life that provided leisure for his private pursuits and literary inclinations. London had been an aberration from self-improvement and self-denial, he concluded. He needed the sobering schedule of study, work, and self-examination that marriage could not provide.

Meanwhile Abigail continued to make caustic remarks about "the Siren" who was undoubtedly skillful in dancing, singing, and drawing, she said, but knew nothing about frugality and running a household on limited funds. In time, she predicted, Louisa would surely bankrupt him. In any event she insisted that her son postpone the marriage.

Abigail's biting words only prompted John Quincy to come to Louisa's defense. He and he alone, he responded, must be accountable for his choice of a wife. If he waited until his mother approved of his selection he "would certainly be doomed to perpetual celibacy."

How well he knew and understood his mother.

Shocked at his reply, and perhaps fearful that she had overplayed her hand, Abigail assured him that whomever he chose would be regarded by her as a daughter.

In the midst of this family tumult over his marriage, John Quincy received notification that President Washington had promoted him from minister resident in the Netherlands to minister plenipotentiary in Portugal with a raise in salary from $4,500 to $9,000. When Louisa learned of his promotion she insisted they set a date for their marriage. She was more than willing to accompany him to Lisbon and even offered to journey to The Hague and marry him there. But her aggressiveness only deepened his concern about marrying her. Her family was already making plans to return to America to straighten out the father's financial affairs and he urged her to go with them and wait for him. A quarrel ensued that almost brought on a complete break between them. But both backed off. "Reason and judgment" returned. Louisa did not press for an immediate wedding, and he conceded that if a ship could be found to take the two of them to Lisbon then he would consent to setting a date. He thought he was playing it safe by making this concession because it was based on his belief that no such vessel could be found, given the precariousness of maritime shipping. But he figured without Johnson, who used what little resources remained to him to arrange to have one of his schooners carry the two to Lisbon. Caught in a net of his own making John Quincy felt honor bound to keep his pledge, although he warned Louisa that she might be disappointed in marrying him. Nevertheless, a promise is a promise, and despite his mounting fears about wedding this headstrong woman, he set out for Lisbon on June 29, 1797, stopping off in London to marry his betrothed.

Back home a most significant political change had taken place. President Washington refused to stand for a third term after the verbal abuse he had received over the Jay Treaty, and John Adams, by the narrow margin of three electoral votes, was elected president of the United States over Thomas Jefferson. The vote was seventy-one to sixty-eight, and since Jefferson was runner-up, according to the original Constitution, he became vice president.

Once inaugurated, President Adams decided to advance his son's career by removing him from the inconsequential post in Lisbon and naming him as the first minister plenipotentiary to the Kingdom of Prussia, where presumably he could continue to provide useful information on events in Europe. It was a clear case of nepotism, which was exactly how John Quincy viewed the appointment. The promotion was degrading and embarrassing, he said. But his father assured him that it was based solely on merit and the needs of the country.

John Quincy and his brother Tom did not reach London until July 12 because of unfavorable Channel winds. He waited an entire day before contacting his fiancée, which Louisa found extremely irritating. If nothing else it should have provided an early warning of what lay ahead in dealing with this frequently troubled and difficult man. But she had made her decision and had no wish to change her mind at this late date. So, on July 26 at the All Hallows Barking Anglican Church near the Tower of London, Louisa Catherine Johnson and John Quincy Adams exchanged vows in the presence of her parents and his brother. The marriage agreement promised a dowry of five hundred pounds but it was never paid due to the collapse of Johnson's enterprises.

It was not exactly a marriage of convenience. They did care for one another, but most probably neither deeply loved the other. Certainly any indication of passion was missing. But it proved to be a workable marriage, what the historian Samuel Flagg Bemis called a "satisfactory union for a good republican family" and one that in time did bring a measure of genuine and abiding love and respect for each of them. John Quincy ultimately decided that he had been "highly favored" in marrying Louisa, more than he really deserved.

At the time both had good reason to marry. John Quincy had just turned thirty years of age, well past the usual age for respectable men in America to marry, and it meant he was finally and completely out from under the thumb of his parents. For Louisa, who was twenty-two, the idea of breaking an engagement was too humiliating even to contemplate. It would be a stigma that would cause lasting pain. Besides, she had decided that John Quincy, despite his many faults, was a real catch, a man who could provide the kind of life she wanted. In addition, they shared many interests and pleasures: both loved literature, music, and the theater. Both enjoyed composing prose and poetry and translating the classics.

And they made an attractive couple. In his youth JQA was a handsome man, as the portrait of him done a year earlier by John Singleton Copley clearly shows. He was smaller than average and of slight build. By the age of thirty a degree of stoutness had already appeared, but his face with its lively eyes, sharp nose, and full lips still marked him as fairly good-looking. Louisa was also small and quite attractive. Dark-haired, bright-eyed, and vivacious, she proved to be an outstanding hostess, which he wanted and needed, as well as an engaging conversationalist in both English and French.

Adams remained in London waiting for the arrival of his credentials and instructions. Once they arrived he, his wife, brother, and servants departed for Berlin in mid-October. Shortly after their arrival, King Frederick William II died, succeeded by Frederick William III, who formally greeted the new minister.

The immediate purpose of Adams's mission to Prussia was to renew and revise the ten-year pacts with Prussia and Sweden and bring them in line with the principles of the Jay Treaty, which necessarily meant abandoning the long-held doctrine of "free ships, free trade." It took a year and a half before Adams successfully completed this peace treaty with Prussia, signed on his thirty-second birthday, July 11, 1799. But he failed to gain a similar treaty with Sweden because of that country's close ties with France at a time when the United States almost declared war against its revolutionary ally. The XYZ Affair, involving French ministers seeking a bribe from their American counterparts, resulted in the suspension of diplomatic relations. In addition the French disapproved of the Jay Treaty and the abandonment of the "free ships, free trade" principle. Soon frigates of the two countries began shooting at one another in what was called a "Quasi-War," but President Adams successfully prevented it from escalating into a full-fledged conflict. Fortunately the five-man French Directory was overthrown by Napoleon Bonaparte on November 9, 1799, and normal diplomatic relations were restored.

JQA also had problems at home in Berlin. During the early years of their marriage Louisa suffered one miscarriage after another—four of them by 1800—and her health remained so frail that it sometimes brought on prolonged spells of melancholy. John Quincy devoted himself to her care and soon found that his affection for her steadily grew.

To help restore Louisa's health he took her for a vacation in Dresden. The holiday had such a beneficial effect on her that the following summer of 1800 they toured the Prussian province of Silesia on the border of Bohemia. They explored the region, visited museums and castles, theaters and galleries, and inspected various business enterprises. At various parties and social events he talked about the towns and cities they had visited and the Silesian people they had met; and he gave detailed descriptions of the literature, economy, history, and politics of the province. In an outburst of literary creativity he wrote up his observations in a series of letters to his brother Tom, who had returned to America, and Tom subsequently published them to critical acclaim, so much so that the *Letters on Silesia* later appeared in Britain and France. It was subsequently translated into German and printed in Prussia as well.

Once Louisa and her husband returned to Berlin their activities were sharply circumscribed because she was again pregnant. There had been so many disappointments in the past that neither John Quincy nor Louisa informed their families in America of her condition lest they be disappointed once more. But disappointment had already visited the Adams family in Massachusetts. In the presidential contest of 1800 John Adams was defeated for reelection by Thomas Jefferson. The Federalist party had split, in part because of Adams's failure to address the nation's grievances and urge war against France. The Republicans won handily, especially in arousing resentment against the Alien and Sedition Acts passed by the Adams administration restricting free speech and attempting to repress political opposition.

The only happy news to reach Abigail and John Adams at this time came when they received word that Louisa had given birth on April 12, 1801, to a healthy boy named George Washington Adams. Two weeks following the birth of his son John Quincy received a notice that his father had recalled him. Rather than see his son dismissed and humiliated by the incoming administration, President Adams, as one of his last official acts, terminated John Quincy's diplomatic career—at least for the moment.

3

From Federalist to Republican

In mid-June 1801 John Quincy, Louisa, and George Washington Adams made their way to Hamburg to set sail for Philadelphia, but not until July 12 did the weather allow their ship to move down the Elbe River to the North Sea. They reached their final destination on September 4, whereupon his wife and son headed for Washington for a reunion with her parents, and he remained in Philadelphia to visit with his literary friends before heading for Quincy to meet his parents, whom he had not seen in seven years.

JQA stopped off along the way to commiserate with Nabby, who was living in New York. Her husband, Colonel William Smith, had virtually deserted her and her children, leaving behind a mountain of debts that eventually landed him in debtors' prison. Another tragedy had occurred the year before when JQA's younger brother Charles died of alcoholism, perhaps the victim of a difficult childhood since he too had been subjected to Abigail's unrelenting demands and criticism.

After spending a short holiday with his parents he decided to set up a private law practice in Boston where he purchased a house in Hanover Square. Not until October 14 did he finally head for Washington to retrieve his family and bring them to Quincy to meet his parents. Naturally Louisa found Abigail quite domineering and a degree of tension always existed between them, but she got along swimmingly with her father-in-law.

John Quincy and his family adapted quickly to life in Boston. He continued his life of writing and studying and soon established a respectable law practice. He gave several public addresses, purchased a pew at the Old Brick Meeting House, and joined the volunteer firemen's organization. However, as much as he loved a life that gave him time for his books, writing, and other "private interests," he found that he missed public service, the sense that his life had "a special meaning." He really aspired to be a statesman who could provide wise leadership for the mass of ordinary citizens, but he had no taste for the life of a politician. He would serve in a public capacity if asked—and most willingly; but he would never put himself forward.

On April 5, 1802, the citizens of Suffolk County, which included Boston, invited him to run on a Federalist ticket as a state senator. Considering how his father was hated by some Federalists in Massachusetts, John Quincy did not expect to win. But when, to his surprise, he defeated his opponent, he chose to believe that his victory had nothing to do with politics and therefore he could serve as an independent.

Once the legislature met in the spring of 1802 he immediately demonstrated that independence. For example, an old friend, the wealthy and very influential Harrison Gray Otis, applied for a bank charter, but since the stock was reserved for a select few, John Quincy opposed it. After a number of such incidents Federalists recognized that his vote could never be counted on and many of them began to regret his election. He subsequently paid a price for his independence. He said he had hoped to initiate some reforms and check some abuses in government, but "I regret to say with little success."

Probably to oust him gracefully from the legislature several Federalists suggested he run for Congress in the fall election of 1802. He had already demonstrated the power of the Adams name on a ticket and they thought he could win the seat and simultaneously vanish from state politics. Without a moment's hesitation he accepted their proposal. Naturally he did not stoop to campaign for the office, and although he won the city of Boston he lost the contest to the Republican incumbent, Dr. William Eustis. The reason for his defeat may well be the fact that Federalists in the surrounding townships stayed home on account of the inclement weather. He lost by 59 votes out of 3,739 cast.

Undeterred by this setback, a number of determined Federalists decided on another route. Both U.S. senators from Massachusetts had to be replaced: one stepped down and the other chose not to seek reelection. When asked about running, JQA jumped at it. He wanted this lofty seat for several reasons: it would provide a secure six-year term with a respectable income; time to devote to writing and studying and practicing law; and an opportunity to assist in directing the nation's future. He found it irresistible.

But this election involved other complications, aside from John Quincy's questionable loyalties as a Federalist. The party itself had split into factions. One, called the Essex Junto, was led by Timothy Pickering, whom President Adams had dismissed from his cabinet for his disloyalty and betrayal. Both father and son loathed Pickering, who was seeking one of the Senate seats. The other faction, united in opposition to Pickering and his friends rather than by any fealty to President Adams, believed that John Quincy could provide them with a vote-getting candidate. Elections to the U.S. Senate at that time were decided in the state legislatures so a private "arrangement" was devised—something John Quincy abominated but did not hesitate to accept—whereby the Essex Junto would have two ballots to elect Pickering. If they failed then the Junto would support JQA. As part of the arrangement Adams pledged that if elected he himself would vote for Pickering for the second Senate seat. As it turned out the Junto failed both times to put Pickering over and John Quincy Adams was elected to the full six-year term. Shortly thereafter, Pickering, with JQA's vote, was elected to the second seat. These two made an unlikely pair of Massachusetts legislators, but it was a satisfying victory all around.

Another cause of celebration occurred when a second son was born to Louisa and her husband on July 4, 1803, and named John Adams II after his grandfather, an event that greatly pleased Abigail, although the child never did resemble the ex-president, physically, intellectually, or emotionally.

The election of JQA to the Senate occurred at the time when the U.S. minister to France, Robert R. Livingston, had completed negotiations for the purchase of Louisiana for $15 million. Once notified of this colossal sale, which virtually doubled the size of the nation, President Jefferson summoned a special session of the Senate to meet on October 17—weeks ahead of the scheduled time—to ratify the treaty. A nationalist to the core and a man who staunchly supported territorial expansion, John Quincy fully intended to vote his approval, even though the Federalist party opposed the treaty on constitutional grounds. He later wrote that the acquisition was "one of the happiest events which had occurred since the adoption of the Constitution." Unfortunately an extended delay caused by his wife's illness prevented him from casting his vote for the treaty. He and his family arrived in Washington on October 20 just moments before the Senate gave its consent, twenty-four to seven. They took up residence at the home of his brother-in-law, Walter Hellen, outside Georgetown, where they remained for the duration of his senatorial tenure. Had Adams actually voted for the treaty he would have been the only Federalist to do so.

When JQA took his seat in the upper house in 1803 the nation consisted of seventeen states represented by thirty-four senators. Some of his colleagues included James A. Bayard of Delaware, Abraham Baldwin of Georgia, John Breckinridge of Kentucky, Samuel Smith of Maryland, William Plumer of New Hampshire, Pierce Butler of South Carolina, and, for a brief period, De Witt Clinton of New York—all presided over by the vice president, Aaron Burr. It was not an especially distinguished collection of public figures, and JQA had little trouble in demonstrating his striking intellectual talents as well as his waywardness as a party loyalist. He remained independent-minded and developed a knack of regularly offending both Federalists and Republicans. For example, he voted against the bill that created the Louisiana Territory, even though he supported the purchase. He insisted that the Constitution be amended to give the purchase legitimacy. His amendment was quickly squelched and the Louisiana bill passed overwhelmingly. The Republicans were annoyed by his obstructionist tactics in arguing for a constitutional amendment, and the Federalists were equally aggravated by his support of the purchase. After only two months in Washington he admitted that his conduct had "given satisfaction to neither side, and both are offended at what they consider a vain and foolish presumption of singularity." He further offended the administration by voting against the removal of the judges impeached by the House of Representatives as well as against the Twelfth Amendment to the Constitution, which provided a much-needed reform of the electoral college.

Back in Quincy good old domineering Abigail was ever ready to provide instructions on his behavior and appearance so that they would not reflect unfavorably on her. "Now I hope you never appear in Senate with a beard two days old, or otherwise make what is called a shabby appearance. . . . I do not wish a Senator to . . . give occasion to the world to ask what kind of mother he had?" He was "slovenly" (her favorite word to describe him) and had no regard for neatness. "You eat too little and study too much," she nagged. Mind that your coat is always brushed.

With the adjournment of Congress in the spring of 1804, Adams spent the summer studying every law passed by the legislature since 1789 and all the Supreme Court decisions. In the fall he watched as Jefferson was overwhelmingly reelected (the treacherous Aaron Burr was replaced by George Clinton as vice president). But within a few months the war between England and France intensified and had a devastating effect on American shipping. The United States tried to maintain its neutrality but its ships and property were regularly seized by both combatants. In the Senate, Adams authored two resolutions condemning the seizures and demanding reparations.

It was during this period of increasing international tension that Adams was offered the Boylston Professorship of Rhetoric and Oratory at Harvard at a salary of $348 per quarter, the gift of a relative, Nicholas Boylston. He was delighted with the offer but insisted on a number of conditions that would allow him to continue as a senator, teach during the summer when Congress was not in session, live outside Cambridge, and be exempt from the declaration of religious conformity required of all faculty. It took many months of negotiations, and not until 1806 did he commence teaching. He loved the idea of beginning the life of a scholar in which he could read his beloved Greek and Roman classics and share his enthusiasm for them with bright and interested under-graduates. He even purchased a house in Boston for $15,000 where he planned to take up residence once his senatorial career ended. The house was located at the corner of present-day Tremont and Boylston streets, and there his third son, Charles Francis Adams, named after JQA's late brother and Francis Dana, was born on August 18, 1807.

JQA's career took a sudden and sharp turn when the British frigate *Leopard*, in search of presumed deserters, attacked the USS frigate *Chesapeake* outside Norfolk, Virginia, and killed three Americans in the skirmish. An angry protest over this violation of U.S. neutrality erupted in the country with demands for an apology and reparations. Adams was particularly outraged and he called upon his Federalist friends to stage a protest meeting. But they refused. So anxious were they to appease Britain, the major source of their very lucrative international trade, that they chose to remain silent rather than protest or retaliate. Whereupon Adams attended a Republican rally and was immediately assigned to a committee to draw up appropriate resolutions. Not unexpectedly that action infuriated Federalists and they denounced him as an turncoat. He realized that his participation in the rally would "displease" his party, but he "could not help it," he said. "My sense of duty shall never yield to the pleasure of party."

In short order one "disloyal" act followed another. Jefferson summoned Congress into session to address the crisis. He sent down a request for an embargo that would prohibit all exports from American ports, and Adams was assigned to a committee to write the legislation. He not only helped fashion the embargo bill but voted for it when it was formally introduced in the Senate, the only Federalist to do so. And that action brought down on him a torrent of abuse from the Federalist press. Was there anything worse than an apostate, a Judas? they asked. To all intents and purposes they effectively read him out of the party. In response he pleaded with his constituents to remember that "private interest must not be put in opposition to public good."

The criticism worsened when the embargo was put into operation. It naturally devastated New England shipping, and Adams suffered unrelenting censure. But it did not faze him in the least. He even proposed a bill to exclude British goods from American ports until they repudiated their unlawful acts on the high seas. Other Federalists, such as his colleague Timothy Pickering, defended British policies and demanded the repeal of the embargo, a demand that won widespread support throughout New England. But it so disturbed Adams that he wrote an open letter to Harrison Gray Otis, one of Pickering's allies, in which he blasted Pickering's arguments as an attempt to coddle the British and win their protection for American commerce. He also ridiculed Pickering's dismissal of the impressment practice (something like nine thousand American seamen were actually impressed by the British) and denounced the claim that England had a "right" to the practice under the rubric of "once an Englishman, always an Englishman."

To make matters infinitely worse John Quincy attended the Republican congressional caucus in Washington on January 23, 1808. It was summoned to choose the party's presidential ticket for the coming election. The ninety congressmen overwhelmingly chose James Madison to head the ticket, and in the balloting for vice president one vote was cast for John Quincy Adams, presumably to reach out to Federalists and establish national unity. But the choice went to George Clinton. Both Republican candidates easily won the election in 1808 over the Federalists, Charles Cotesworth Pinckney and Rufus King.

Abigail was thunderstruck. She could scarcely believe that her own son would do such a despicable thing. It "staggered my belief," she wrote him; it was a violation of "your principles," to which John Quincy replied, "I could wish to please my parents—but my duty I *must* do."

By this time Senator Adams had become a pariah in his own state and region and no one doubted that his days in Congress were numbered. As a matter of fact he advanced the time for choosing his successor. Rather than be humiliated by dismissal, Adams resigned his office on June 8, 1808, informing the legislature in his letter that "I now restore to you the trust committed to my charge."

Freed from his legislative responsibilities Adams now returned to his books, his law practice, and his teaching at Harvard. He even pleaded before the Supreme Court in the famous case *Fletcher v. Peck*, arguing for the defendant.

While in Washington he decided to attend President James Madison's inauguration, and two days later he received a message that the president wished to see him. It seems the czar of Russia, Alexander I, had requested an American minister, and Madison offered the post to Adams. Once again JQA seized the opportunity to serve his country and immediately accepted the offer. He had come to enjoy public life and although it would mean giving up teaching at Harvard the appointment would return him to a life of diplomacy as well as restore him to his country's service. In addition it would provide a steady salary of $9,000 per annum. He was expected to serve as minister plenipotentiary for at least three or four years.

Naturally Abigail disapproved. "I do not wish to see you under existing circumstances any other than the private citizen you now are," she declared, which may have been another reason for his accepting the position so readily.

Because he wanted to raise his children the same way he had been reared—one would think he had more sense than that—and because of his own earlier experience in Russia, he decided to leave his two older children, George and John II, in the United States and place them in the care of his aunt and her husband, Mary (Abigail's sister) and Richard Cranch. His brother Thomas acted as general supervisor of their education. When the couple died in 1811 the children lived with another aunt and her husband, Elizabeth (also one of Abigail's sisters) and Stephen Peabody, who lived in New Hampshire where the boys went to school. Only the youngest, Charles Francis, would accompany Adams and his wife to Russia.

Louisa strongly objected to leaving her eight-year-old George and six-year-old John II at home. Indeed she and her husband quarreled incessantly over the education of the boys but in this instance John Quincy would not give way. In reluctantly accepting his decision she did something she regretted for the rest of her life and she never really forgave him. Her reaction can well be imagined when the lives of both George and John II later ended in tragedy.

But the Senate of the United States had different ideas about this mission and passed a resolution calling it expensive and unnecessary. Nevertheless Madison insisted, and in view of the swiftly developing events occurring in Napoleonic Europe the Senate reconsidered and on June 27, 1809, confirmed Adams as the U.S. minister plenipotentiary to Russia by the vote of nineteen to seven. Five Federalists in the chamber, including the two from Massachusetts, voted against the nomination and were joined by two Republicans who still thought the entire idea a waste of money.

On August 5 Adams closed his house in Boston and together with his wife and son; Louisa's sister Catherine; Nabby's son, William Steuben Smith, who would serve as private secretary; and several servants drove to the wharf at Charleston where they boarded the *Horace* and headed for St. Petersburg.

It took almost three months to complete the journey and they arrived at their destination on October 23, 1809, just before the winter closed in and froze the Kronstadt harbor, sealing off access to the outside world until the following May. For JQA his tenure as American minister to the court of Alexander I was a series of personal successes. He had developed into a first-rate diplomat on account of his intellectual gifts, including his knowledge of history, literature, and science, his linguistic abilities, his lively conversation, his tactful conduct at all times, and his general attractiveness at parties and other social events. But for Louisa their sojourn in Russia was one long agony as she tormented herself with guilt feelings about the children she had "deserted." And she never hesitated to communicate her feelings to her husband and friends and family back home. "I do not like the place or the people," she complained.

Quite remarkably, Alexander and John Quincy hit it off immediately and they became frequent walking companions, speaking fluently in French about developing events in Europe and about life in the United States, which fascinated the young thirty-two-year-old monarch. It was another reason for Adams's overall success in Russia.

Adams enjoyed his post so much that when, a year later, the president offered an appointment on the bench of the Supreme Court, he turned it down. He gave as his reason the fact that Louisa was pregnant again and could not survive a prolonged sea voyage; but his real concern involved the fact that he detested the drudgery of the law. He much preferred literature and even the nastiness of politics to a life of writs, subpoenas, and contending interpretations of state and national statutes and constitutions. Worse, the salary of an associate justice came to a paltry $3,500. He made almost triple that amount as minister. So he thanked Madison for his gesture of confidence but was forced to turn him down due to the "peculiar circumstances" of his wife's condition.

Louisa gave birth to her first daughter on August 12, 1811. The child was named after her mother, Louisa Catherine, and Czar Alexander offered to serve as godfather. The offer was refused and the month-old baby was baptized by the chaplain of the British ambassador on September 9 in an Anglican service. John Quincy was ecstatic. He admitted in his diary that his marriage had not always been "without its trials" and dissensions. But on the whole, he said, Louisa was a dutiful and faithful wife. And now that he had a beautiful daughter he felt truly blessed.

His diplomatic successes began when he urged the czar to intervene and request the release of captured American ships held by Denmark. The Danish government agreed and the ships were permitted to leave the country, for which the administration formally thanked the czar for his intervention. Adams also protected the rights of his countrymen in Russian ports, despite the restrictions on neutral trade that Napoleon had imposed over the countries under his domination. Since Russia was allied to France, Alexander went out of his way to oblige JQA's request, and this action signaled his intention to dissociate himself from the French emperor, a fact made explicit in a ukase issued in December 1810.

The tension between the two nations reached a climax when Napoleon massed his Grand Army of over half a million men along the eastern frontier of his empire and on June 25, 1812, invaded Russia. A week earlier the United States, constantly humiliated by British impressment of American seamen, the seizure of ships, the violation of neutral rights, and the refusal to withdraw from military posts along the Canadian frontier as required by the Peace

Treaty of Paris that ended the Revolution, declared war against England on June 19.

In the midst of these extraordinary events the Adams family was devastated by the sudden death of their youngest child and only daughter on September 15, 1812. Not surprisingly, it deepened the father's interest in religion. Because there were no Protestant churches in Russia that he could regularly attend, Adams took up the study of the Bible and became something of a biblical scholar, reading widely and deeply about the roots and theology of Christianity. "Religious sentiments become from day to day more constantly habitual to my mind," he wrote in his diary. "They are perhaps too often seen in this journal." He also began the study of astronomy, the differences between the English and American units of measurement, and the new French metric system that Napoleon was imposing on Europe.

Adams found himself in an awkward position now that France had invaded Russia while his own country had declared war against England. Yet by this time his diplomatic skills had been so deftly honed that he maintained a proper balance in his relations with the Russian government and the other foreign diplomats. His friendship with the czar remained strong, so much so that Alexander offered his services in mediating the differences between the United States and England and was willing to support American demands for freedom of the seas. Without authorization, or consultation with his superiors in Washington, Adams promptly accepted the offer.

President Madison also accepted it. After a series of military defeats on land and sea, he was eager for peace and appointed Albert Gallatin, former secretary of the treasury, and Senator James Bayard of Delaware to meet with Adams in St. Petersburg under Alexander's supervision and conclude a treaty with Britain to end the war. Unfortunately Great Britain rejected the offer. It had no intention of negotiating under Russian mediation since Russia would surely favor the American position on the question of freedom of the seas.

Meanwhile, Napoleon's troops proved extremely vulnerable to the Russian winter and army and were slowly driven back across the frozen landscape. Only about thirty thousand of the Grand Army managed to survive the ordeal and recross the frontier. Napoleon himself fled back to Paris as fast as he could travel and later resigned his throne as his empire fell apart.

By the time Gallatin and Bayard reached St. Petersburg it was already known that England would not consent to negotiations in Russia. But then Lord Castlereagh, the British foreign secretary, offered to meet the Americans in London. When that suggestion proved unacceptable to the U.S. delegation the British agreed to negotiate in Göteborg, Sweden, but later changed it to the medieval town of Ghent in what is now Belgium. To improve American representation, President Madison added two additional commissioners: the Speaker of the House of Representatives, Henry Clay of Kentucky, and Jonathan Russell, former chargé d'affaires in London and newly appointed minister to Sweden, all under the chairmanship of John Quincy Adams.

At this stage of his career Adams had developed a sharply defined sense of what he considered essential for the United States with respect to its foreign policy. Independence and union formed the core of his thinking. Connected with this was his firm belief in what was later termed "Manifest Destiny." "The whole continent of North America," he told his father, "appears to be destined by Divine Providence to be peopled by one nation, speaking one language, professing one general system of religious and political principles, and accustomed to one general tenor of social usages and customs. For the common happiness of them all, for their peace and prosperity, I believe it indispensable that they should be associated in one federal Union." In addition his many years abroad had taught him that if his country hoped to preserve its independence it must steer clear of involvement in European affairs. Thus, union, independence, neutrality, and continental expansion summed up his political and ideological convictions, all expressed at different times and different occasions by his ardent and sweeping nationalism.

JQA and Jonathan Russell were the first U.S. commissioners to arrive in Ghent on June 24 to begin deliberations with the British. They were soon joined by the other three, and it did not take long for their differences in personality and temperament to surface and cause trouble. Five men of different backgrounds, interests, and personalities, living and dining together each day to save money, were bound to cause friction—and it arose almost immediately. Because of what he considered the inadequacies and limitations of the others, Adams regularly showed the unpleasant side of his character. He finally withdrew from dining with them, complaining that they smoked cigars and drank bad wine until all hours of the night and wasted precious time. This affront disturbed the others, but Clay, ever the beguiling and affable politician, managed to smooth things over and convince Adams to rejoin the common dining table. Still, the fact that the others stayed up late at night noisily playing cards annoyed John Quincy to distraction. Sometimes their parties did not end until 4 A.M., the very time he rose to begin the day's work. Such irritants caused him to admit that he was not the "master" of himself and that he allowed his annoyance and aggravation to erupt into verbal tirades. Particularly hurtful to him were the objections of the others to drafts he composed to be submitted to their British counterparts. If any one of them objected to his proposal, he said, the others agreed with the objection, but let him object to a draft written by any one of them "and my objection is utterly unavailing."

Intellectual pride. One of JQA's towering problems in life.

The British delegation consisted of Admiral Lord Gambier, a minor aristocrat, Henry Goulburn, a member of Parliament, and Dr. William Adams, an expert in international and maritime law. They were all second rate, taking their orders directly from London, and vastly inferior to their American counterparts. The major British diplomats were assembling in Vienna to work out a peace treaty with France after Napoleon had resigned as emperor and been exiled to Elba. With the allied powers of Russia, Austria, Prussia, and England now in full control of Europe and the British poised to send Wellington's veteran troops to end the American war, all but Henry Clay among the U.S. delegation gave little hope of concluding a peace treaty at Ghent.

They waited six weeks for the British delegation to arrive. Not until August 8, 1814, did the first meeting with Gambier, Goulburn, and Dr. Adams take place at the Hotel des Pays Bas. John Quincy told Louisa that "scarcely an hour passes without accumulating evidence to my mind that our antagonists are fully resolved not to make peace this time."

The problems were three, as he told his father: boundary, fisheries, and "the Indian savages." Actually, there were others, such as impressment of seamen and the freedom of the seas. Secretary of State James Monroe had instructed the U.S. delegation to insist on the impressment issue, something the British stoutly refused to do. By the same token the British wanted an independent Indian territory established in the upper Midwest as a barrier between the United States and Canada, and complete access to the Great Lakes, an issue the Americans, especially Clay, adamantly rejected. In no way would the Americans yield an inch of U.S. territory.

The position of the U.S. delegation was gravely damaged by news from home. The British had begun a three-pronged general invasion of the United States from Canada, the Chesapeake, and the Gulf. Although the invasion from Canada stalled, the expedition into the Chesapeake resulted in the capture of Washington and the burning of the Capitol, the White House, and other governmental buildings.

At Ghent the diplomatic situation improved somewhat when, at Clay's insistence, the American commissioners agreed that Britain would never give up the right of impressment and that they should disregard their instructions on this point. Gallatin passed the suggestion along to Monroe, who acted on it promptly and withdrew that requirement from his instructions to the delegation. Similarly the British backed off from their demand for an Indian buffer state. From that point a peaceful settlement began moving forward.

Undoubtedly JQA's single most important contribution to the negotiations came with his insistence that the two countries accept the status quo ante bellum, with all other contending issues subject to future negotiation, including boundary and the fisheries question. The British consented and after these many months of discussion the final treaty was signed on Christmas eve 1814. As Adams exchanged copies of the document with Lord Gambier, he said that he "hoped it would be the last treaty of peace between Great Britain and the United States." A beautiful touch, one subsequently realized.

Not much later came the heartening news that General Andrew Jackson and his troops had devastated Wellington's veterans at New

Orleans, thus providing Americans with the colossal military victory they so desperately wanted and needed.

The British insisted that the terms of the treaty would not go into effect until both countries ratified the document. The treaty did not reach Washington until February 14. The Senate unanimously ratified it three days later, and that is when the war ended, not Christmas eve as frequently and erroneously stated.

Prior to the conclusion of the negotiations, Adams had decided to end his ministry to Russia and return to the United States. He had long since completed the three- or four-year term he had agreed to and felt it was time to go home. He therefore requested his recall. He also instructed Louisa to close out their affairs in St. Petersburg, sell the furniture, bid their friends and associates farewell, and together with Charles Francis join him in Paris, where he would wait for her. Meanwhile Napoleon escaped from Elba and returned to France to begin his Hundred Days reign. Shortly thereafter Louisa and Charles Francis arrived in Paris, having endured a harrowing overland journey across war-torn Europe. Then, to his surprise, Adams was notified on May 7 of his appointment as minister plenipotentiary to Great Britain where he was directed to meet with Clay and Gallatin and negotiate a treaty of commerce. The opportunity to serve his country in a position of possibly enormous influence far outweighed his desire to return home. So he accepted the post, summoned his sons George and John II to join him, and moved to London where he presented his credentials to the Prince Regent on June 8, 1815.

The family was reunited shortly thereafter when John and Louisa met their two oldest sons, whom they had not seen in nearly six years and hardly recognized. JQA, without giving it a second thought, immediately subjected George, now fourteen, and John II, twelve, to the kind of rigorous life and education he had endured: rising early to begin the day with Bible study, followed by lessons in Latin and Greek and French. But being the gloomy worrier he had become, John Quincy convinced himself that most probably none of his children would "ever answer my hopes." Pray God that "none of them ever realizes my fears."

The negotiations for a new treaty of commerce took place during Napoleon's last struggle for survival. Under the circumstances Britain had no intention of agreeing to any alteration of its major policies and what resulted was a commercial convention (so-called because of the limited extent of its provisions), which merely confirmed existing practices. As usual Adams was his testy self on occasion and many of the sore points between the two nations—impressment, Indian trade, blockades, colonial trade restrictions—were left to future negotiations. But the convention did open the British East Indies to American ships, prohibit discriminatory duties, and provide commercial terms on the basis of "most favored nation." It was signed on July 3, 1815, just a few weeks after the Battle of Waterloo, which sent Napoleon into permanent exile on St. Helena island.

For the remainder of his tour as minister to Great Britain, Adams went about his usual duties by attempting to strengthen friendly relations between the two countries. He got along well with the prime minister, Lord Liverpool, and the foreign secretary, Lord Castlereagh, and he also cultivated a friendship with George Canning, one of the rising luminaries in British politics. Naturally he regularly attended dinners, receptions, and the theater. He welcomed visiting American dignitaries and dutifully reported his observations and opinions to Washington. He also called British attention to any unpleasant incident that took place along the U.S.-Canadian frontier, and on January 25, 1816, acting on instructions from the secretary of state, proposed a reciprocal reduction of armaments on the Great Lakes. He repeated the proposal on March 21. Castlereagh responded favorably and it subsequently resulted in the Rush-Bagot Agreement of April 28–29, 1817, which limited naval armament on the lakes to a particular number and size of ships. As the diplomatic historian Samuel Flagg Bemis has pointed out, it was "the first reciprocal naval disarmament in the history of international relations."

About the same time Adams made this proposal, one of the visiting Americans to England brought news that James Monroe had been elected president in the fall election of 1816 and intended to name Adams as secretary of state. Of course these were only rumors but such an appointment made a great deal of sense. Who was more qualified than Adams to head the State Department? There was no one, except possibly Albert Gallatin, but he was foreign born, and the office of the secretary traditionally led directly to the presidency. For that reason Henry Clay fancied himself as secretary even though he had only limited diplomatic experience. Still, he deeply resented Monroe's decision to invite Adams to head his cabinet.

The letter of appointment arrived in London on April 16, 1817. Former President John Adams urged his son "to accept it without hesitation," and his mother added her recommendation since it virtually guaranteed his election to the presidency. People, she wrote him, were already beginning to say that you are "worthy to preside over the Counsels of a Great Nation."

John Quincy welcomed the advice and Monroe's invitation, which he accepted with thanks. It took him several weeks to wind up his affairs before he and his family were ready to set sail for America. "I bid adieu to London," he wrote on June 10 as he departed the British capital. And then with a sigh, he added, "in all probability forever."

Five days later the Adams family boarded the ship *Washington* and headed home.

4

Secretary of State

John Quincy Adams is arguably the greatest secretary of state to serve that office. His negotiating skills and diplomatic insights were mainly responsible for the transformation of the United States into a transcontinental nation, an action that guaranteed the emergence of this country as a world power. Moreover, it was his statesmanship that led directly to the formulation of one of the most basic and fundamental precepts of U.S. foreign policy, namely the Monroe Doctrine. In effect he established what Samuel Flagg Bemis has called the foundations of American foreign policy.

When JQA and his family arrived back in New York City on August 6, 1817, the American people had already begun to recognize his diplomatic genius. He was feted and honored for helping to bring the War of 1812 to an end without loss of territory or honor. A dinner given to welcome him in New York was presided over by Governor De Witt Clinton and he was escorted to the affair by John Jacob Astor, whose fur-trading interests in the far West provided an added U.S. claim to the entire Pacific Northwest, a claim challenged by the British.

Adams rented a house in Washington (his three sons were left with relatives in Quincy) that allowed him to walk to work each day to the State Department building on 17th and G Streets, which later moved to 15th Street and Pennsylvania Avenue, the corner of the present Treasury building. Walking and swimming were two of his favorite recreations and he frequently swam in the Potomac as both secretary and president. In assuming this new office he took a substantial cut in salary. He received $3,500, which Congress increased to $6,000 in 1819.

Aside from formulating policy and dealing with diplomats from around the world, he consulted with the president on a daily basis, conducted an extensive correspondence with dozens of U.S. ministers and hundreds of consuls abroad, maintained and managed government documents, supervised the Patent Office and census, issued passports, arranged the printing of the Records of the Constitutional Convention of 1787 and the Secret Journals of the Continental Congress, and ran what he found to be a chaotic office that he quickly reformed into an efficient operation.

One of his first assignments was a request from Congress that he prepare a report on the standards for weights and measures current in the United States. Ever the diligent scholar he spent days, months, and years researching (he asked each state to submit its regulations) and writing the work, and he not only provided a penetrating analysis of the subject but delved into its history and philosophy as well. The *Report of the Secretary of State on Weights and Measures* submitted and published in 1822 is, in the words of Samuel Flagg Bemis, "a sadly neglected classic in the historiography of modern science." It praised the French metric system and demonstrated the need for a uniform and universal standard. Adams himself thought the *Report* worthy of "the remembrance of my children," more so than anything else he had written. But Congress, alas, did not act on it.

In the two terms of his administration President Monroe worked very closely with his secretary of state. "They were made for each other," commented Thomas Jefferson. They not only respected each other but kept one another informed of their decisions and actions. When Adams took office there were nine European countries with representatives in Washington. With the U.S. recognition by the Monroe administration of the independence of new countries in Latin America, that number increased to fifteen.

Adams was replaced as minister to England by Richard Rush of Pennsylvania, who had served as interim secretary of state in the months prior to John Quincy's arrival in Washington. Rush completed the negotiations initiated by Adams that resulted in the Rush-Bagot Agreement of 1817. From this beginning Adams fully intended to build a new era of relations with Great Britain by negotiating many of the issues left unresolved at Ghent.

First off was the fisheries question, which dealt with the "liberty" of Americans to fish off the Grand Banks and dry and cure their catch on the nearby islands. In the Treaty of Paris that ended the Revolution, John Adams had negotiated what he believed was an American "right" to fish in this area and his son now felt obligated to preserve it. JQA's arguments convinced Lord Castlereagh to renew this "liberty" on certain stipulated coasts of British possessions on condition that the United States would renounce such liberty on all other coasts.

Another issue that went back to his father's diplomacy involved the boundary between the United States and Canada in the northwest. With the purchase of Louisiana, the Lewis and Clark expedition, and the trading posts of John Jacob Astor's American Fur Company, the undefined boundary between the two countries now extended from the Great Lakes to the Pacific Ocean and needed to be drawn precisely. The Treaty of Ghent skirted the issue by leaving its settlement to a future commission. Monroe therefore decided to send a U.S. warship to the mouth of the Columbia River and take possession of the entire area. Fortunately, Castlereagh was attempting to cement relations with the United States in view of the formation of the Holy Alliance in Europe, which he opposed and which was intent on reestablishing monarchs overthrown during the Napoleonic era. He therefore wished to avoid any semblance of a confrontation with the United States. So he suggested that a mixed commission be named to settle the entire boundary question from the Lake of the Woods north of the Mississippi River to the Pacific. Meanwhile Adams instructed Richard Rush to intimate to Castlereagh that while the U.S. had no concern with the affairs of Europe, Africa, and Asia he expected England to respect extension of "our natural dominions of North America." He hoped a favorable response could also lead to an exchange of views about the newly independent republics of South America, inasmuch as the Holy Alliance seemed determined to help King Ferdinand VII of Spain regain control of those republics. Thanks to the French invasion of Spain under the auspices of the Holy Alliance, Ferdinand had only recently been restored to his throne.

Adams drew up the instructions and proposals relative to the questions of boundary, fisheries, impressment, freedom of the seas, and the demands of slave owners for compensation for property seized from them during the War of 1812 that would be addressed, and he directed Albert Gallatin, the U.S. minister to France, to join Rush in London to assist in resolving these issues with Great Britain. What ultimately resulted was the Convention of 1818 in which the forty-ninth parallel was drawn from the Lake of the Woods to the Rocky Mountains. The territory west of the mountains—what came to be called the Oregon Country—would be jointly occupied for ten years with the further stipulation that the agreement could be renewed every ten years thereafter if both countries consented. In accepting this boundary the United States was rewarded with full access to the Mississippi River and a stretch of territory in northern Michigan and Minnesota that included the rich Mesabi Range of iron ore. The fisheries compromise was included by which Adams agreed that the United States would "desist from the liberty of fishing and of curing and drying fish, within the British jurisdiction *generally*, upon condition that it shall be secured as a permanent right." In other words, as the biographer Lynn Hudson Parsons has noted, the British would maintain the general principle but yield the substance. By this agreement American fisherman continued to enjoy and profit from some of the best fishing grounds available in British North America without Great Britain receiving reciprocal rights from the United States. Unfortunately the question of impressment was not resolved at this time. As for the issue of slave property claims, this was turned over to a third party: Adams's good friend Alexander, the czar of Russia, who subsequently decided the question in favor of the United States.

This Convention of 1818 benefited both countries in terms of their respective diplomatic goals: Britain no longer worried about any threat from the United States concerning its interests in North America, and the United States now pursued its expansionist aims to both the south and the west without fear of British intervention.

It was during the negotiations leading to the Convention that Abigail Adams contracted typhoid fever and died on October 18, 1818. JQA did not return home to comfort his mother during her illness nor did he attend her funeral, much to the distress of relatives and friends. His biographer Paul Nagel suggests that it was another mark of his resentment toward his mother's "dominating ways." Whatever the truth, Louisa made excuses for him by explaining that he was involved in difficult and important questions of state. Indeed that was true. His concern for the safety and continued expansion of the United States rarely left his mind. And at the moment he had his eye on Florida.

The Madison-Monroe administrations had long sought to crowd Spain out of its possessions in East and West Florida. In 1810 and again in 1812 President Madison authorized the seizure of two segments of West Florida, claiming they were portions of the Louisiana Purchase. It remained for Monroe to swallow the rest. The occasion for the action was the invasion of frontier settlements in Georgia and Alabama by Seminole Indians. After attacking and killing Americans the Indians retreated back into Florida where they felt safe from pursuit and reprisal. To end this intolerable situation the administration authorized General Andrew Jackson to lead an army "across the Florida line" and strike the Seminoles "within its limits." They have "long violated our rights," Monroe told the general, "& insulted our national character." They cannot kill our citizens with impunity.

In a series of engagements Jackson not only shattered Indian resistance, killed many Seminole chiefs and warriors, and destroyed their villages but he seized Pensacola and St. Marks, raised the American flag over both Spanish towns, and executed two British nationals, Alexander Arbuthnot and Robert Ambrister, for arming the Indians and encouraging their assaults on American settlements. This act of aggression and military seizure of Florida had the makings of a monumental diplomatic crisis for the United States with both Spain and England.

The administration rightly feared repudiating Jackson because of the general's enormous popularity throughout the country. All the members of the cabinet, save John Quincy Adams, argued against

Jackson and recommended that his conduct be investigated by a military tribunal. Indeed they felt he deserved a censure at the very least. They also insisted on the restoration of Florida to Spain.

Only Adams defended Jackson. He argued that the general was justified by his action in that Spain was unable to police its territory and prevent rampaging "savages" from killing American citizens. At cabinet meetings, he reported in his journal, he was constantly obliged "to oppose the unanimous opinions of the President, the Secretary of the Treasury [William H.] Crawford, the Secretary of War [John C.] Calhoun, and the Attorney-General [William] Wirt. . . . My principle is that everything he [Jackson] did was *defensive;* that as such it was neither war against Spain nor violation of the Constitution."

Ultimately the president accepted Adams's argument and instructed him to inform the Spanish ambassador, Luis de Onís, that although Jackson had acted on his own authority he would not be censured, and that Florida would be returned as soon as Spain stationed an adequate military force in the area to protect Americans from further Indian attack. Adams then convinced Onís that the best way to prevent future military incursions would be for Spain to sell the province to the United States.

Onís may have been reluctant to accept Adams's logic, but he wisely perceived that a greater problem existed between the two nations, namely the settlement of the western boundary of Louisiana so that its Texas and Mexican territories would be protected from further U.S. aggression.

When the French sold Louisiana to the United States the western and northern boundaries were not defined and some Americans claimed that Texas was included in the purchase and they wanted it occupied. Onís therefore suggested that Spain might be willing to cede the indefensible Florida province in return for a settlement of Louisiana's western boundary. Ever the expansionist, Adams expressed a willingness to negotiate the matter and suggested the Rio Grande as the boundary; Onís countered with the Mississippi. Finally the secretary issued what he called an "ultimatum" in which he recommended a line from the Sabine River at the Gulf of Mexico (the present border between the states of Texas and Louisiana),

zigzagging northward to the forty-first parallel, and then running
straight west to the Pacific Ocean. In effect such a line would trans-
form the United States into a transcontinental power. If these terms
were unacceptable, said Adams, he would break off the negotiations.

In the meantime Adams sent a detailed set of instructions to
George W. Erving, the U.S. minister to Spain, to be delivered to the
Spanish government in Madrid, a copy of which was released to the
Washington press. Bemis has called this document the "greatest state
paper of John Quincy Adams's diplomatic career." In it the secretary
justified the invasion of Spanish territory and the executions of
Arbuthnot and Ambrister, and he called upon Spain to adequately
police this "derelict province" or cede it to the United States. "The
President," he declared, "will neither inflict punishment, nor pass a
censure on General Jackson" since his conduct was "founded in the
purest patriotism . . . as well as the first law of nature—self defense."

These carefully worded and skillfully argued instructions not
only neutralized British resentment for the killing of its nationals
but convinced Spain to come to an agreement.

The negotiations consumed an enormous amount of time and
energy but the resulting Adams-Onís or Transcontinental Treaty—
signed on February 22, 1819, and ratified two days later by the Senate—established the western boundary of the Louisiana Purchase
along a line starting at the Sabine River, moving northward along
the Red and Arkansas Rivers to the forty-second parallel (the present northern boundary of California, Nevada, and Utah), and thence
due west to the Pacific Ocean. Spain also surrendered its claims to
the Pacific Northwest to the United States. In return the United
States formally abandoned its claim to Texas but received Florida
for $5,000 to be paid to satisfy American claims against Spain.

The Spanish government delayed acting on the treaty until February 1821 at which time a final exchange of ratifications occurred
that brought the negotiations to a successful conclusion. The treaty,
Bemis contends, "was the greatest diplomatic victory won by any
single individual in the history of the United States." JQA quite
agreed. "The Florida Treaty," he wrote late in life, "was the most
important incident in my life, and the most successful negotiation
ever consummated by the Government of this Union."

Adams also turned his attention to the question of the independence of Latin America, a problem exacerbated by the Speaker of the House, Henry Clay. Angered by the loss of the position he craved, Clay used every opportunity to embarrass the administration—and most especially John Quincy Adams. His rancor first surfaced when he noticed that Adams had made a serious mistake in the Transcontinental Treaty. The secretary had allowed two enormous tracts of land that had only recently been granted to Spanish noblemen to remain as part of the treaty, and remain valid even after the United States took possession of Florida. It was quite unlike Adams to stumble so badly, but with the assistance of the French ambassador, Baron Jean-Guillaume Hyde de Neuville, he convinced Onís to correct the treaty. Luckily the Spanish government agreed to the alteration.

A second opportunity for Clay to embarrass the administration occurred over the revolutionary movements that had occurred in South America. In 1821 on the floor of the House he demanded that the United States, as the beacon of freedom to the world, recognize these liberated governments. A resolution to that effect was passed by the House promising full support in any action the administration would take on the issue. Adams deeply regretted the resolution because it might permanently stall the Transcontinental Treaty still waiting to be ratified. Fortunately it did not. The ratifications went forward, whereupon Monroe sent Congress a special message proposing the establishment of diplomatic relations with the new Latin American republics. Congress gave its consent on May 4, 1822, by appropriating $100,000 for the creation of diplomatic agencies with the several countries. Accordingly the Republic of Colombia was recognized on June 19, Mexico on December 12, 1822, Chile and Argentina on January 27, 1823, Brazil on May 26, 1824, the Federation of Central American States on August 4, 1824, and Peru on May 2, 1826.

It was hoped that recognition of these new republics by the United States would encourage Europe not to meddle in American affairs, just as the United States would steer clear of European concerns. American neutrality was a cardinal doctrine to Adams, and to emphasize the point he used the occasion of a Fourth of July oration in 1821 to establish it as forcefully as he knew how. He delivered the oration from the rostrum of the House of Representatives in which he faced his audience dressed in the robe of a university professor. Staring intently at the crowd seated before him, he declared that the United States would always be "the well-wisher to the freedom and independence of all" nations but that it must not go "abroad in search of monsters to destroy" by enlisting under banners other "than our own." That, to him, would inaugurate America's search for "dominion and power" in the world and would ultimately result in the loss of our own "freedom and independence."

Besides wanting the United States to remain neutral in foreign conflicts, Adams desired the expansion of this country westward across the continent without European interference; at the same time he advocated a noncolonization policy in which South America would remain free of future subjugation by foreign powers. In a celebrated conversation Adams had on January 26, 1821, with the British minister in Washington, Stratford Canning, he expressed the hope that Britain had finally concluded "that there would be neither policy nor profit in caviling with us about territory on this North American continent."

"And in this," Canning replied, "you include our northern provinces on this Continent?"—meaning Canada of course.

"No," Adams shot back, "there the boundary is marked, and we have no disposition to encroach upon it. Keep what is yours, but leave the rest of the continent to us."

"The whole system of modern colonization," he remarked to Canning on another occasion, "is an abuse of government and it is time that it should come to an end." In fact he thought that the United States and Great Britain might "compare their ideas and purposes together, with a view to the accommodation of great interests upon which they have hitherto differed."

Did he mean concluding an alliance, asked Canning.

No, not at all, came the response. Americans wished to remain aloof from European problems and politics. What he had in mind was an agreement on neutral rights, commerce, impressment, and the slave trade.

This policy of noncolonization took sharper focus when it became increasingly apparent that France might assist Spain in winning back its former South American colonies—and with military force if necessary. England regarded such a development as extremely prejudicial to its own commercial enterprises. At that point the new secretary for foreign affairs, George Canning, a cousin of Stratford Canning, discovered Adams's remark about an agreement on "ideas and purposes" among the diplomatic papers left by his predecessor. He subsequently asked Richard Rush a very pointed question. "What do you think your Government would say to going hand in hand with England" and issuing a joint declaration of policy against the recovery of Spain's colonies in America. Of course Rush could not give a direct answer but said he would communicate Canning's suggestion to Washington.

When Monroe received Rush's dispatches about Canning's proposal he was immediately inclined to accept it. After all the British navy would enforce the declaration, and a policy of noninterference in American affairs would be established. But another thought gave him pause. By accepting Canning's proposal it would mean a serious departure from George Washington's dictum against "entangling alliances" with foreign powers. Should this be an exception? Monroe could not decide, so he turned to two former presidents, his friends and fellow Virginians, Thomas Jefferson and James Madison.

Jefferson strongly urged him to accept. It would revolutionize America, he responded, and keep out all foreign nations and prevent them from interfering in our affairs. And if any war ensued, Great Britain would be our ally. Madison seconded Jefferson's approval. "With the British power and navy combined with our own we have nothing to fear from the rest of the nations and in the great struggle of the Epoch between liberty and despotism, we owe it to ourselves to sustain the former in this hemisphere at least."

At the same time Monroe pondered Canning's proposal, the Russian minister to the U.S., Baron von Tuyll, presented Adams with a note from Czar Alexander that expressed satisfaction with American neutrality and implied that if the United States abandoned that policy, the Holy Alliance, of which he was spokesman, would support

France in attempting to recover the Latin American colonies for Spain.

At a cabinet meeting called by Monroe to consider Canning's proposal John Quincy Adams immediately registered his disagreement with accepting it. In view of the czar's note, he said, it affords "a very suitable and convenient opportunity for us to take our stand against the Holy Alliance and at the same time to decline the overture of Great Britain. It would be more candid, as well as more dignified, to avow our principles explicitly to Russia and France, than to come in as a cock-boat in the wake of the British man-of-war."

A cockboat in the wake of the British man-of-war! Precisely. Everyone around the cabinet table agreed. Several days later Adams went on to suggest to the president and cabinet members that the United States should openly declare the principles on which this government was founded and that, while rejecting any idea of spreading those principles elsewhere by force of arms, this nation expected and hoped that Europe would also refrain from propagating its principles in this hemisphere or "subjugate by force any part of these continents to their will."

What Adams had done was advance the ideas of noncolonization and nonintervention by Europe (or any other country or continent) in the New World, the two basic concepts that would form the core of the later Monroe Doctrine. Adams suggested advancing these ideas in a series of diplomatic dispatches, but Monroe decided to include them in his annual message to Congress and in that way lay them before the entire world.

The message was delivered to Congress on December 2, 1823, and much of the language on foreign policy was drafted by Adams. It stated that the American continents can no longer "be considered as subjects for future colonization by any European Power," that in "wars of the European powers, in matters pertaining to themselves, we have never taken any part, nor does it comport with our policy, so to do." Furthermore, the United States would consider any attempt by Europe "to extend their system to any portion of this Hemisphere, as dangerous to our peace and safety. With the existing Colonies or dependencies of any European power, we have not interfered, and shall not interfere."

With the acceptance and publication of these views on American foreign policy, and through the dynamic force of his reason, John Quincy Adams had, in the words of Samuel Flagg Bemis, "prevailed" over Monroe, over ex–Presidents Jefferson and Madison, and over the entire cabinet. For himself and his country, it was a magnificent triumph.

5

The Election of 1824–25

The rented home of the Adams family on 4½ and F Streets became something of a social center in Washington. Elizabeth Monroe was semi-invalid and avoided public appearances, so Louisa became a kind of surrogate hostess. And she was expert at it. Adams himself kept up his several interests and supervised the education of his sons, none of whom pleased the demanding father. When John II and Charles Francis performed poorly at Harvard, he refused to allow them to visit the family for the Christmas holiday. "I could take no satisfaction in seeing you" was his searing response to their request. Shades of Abigail. Actually, he was a worse parent than his mother. He himself enjoyed far more freedom growing up than he ever allowed his sons. He was always after them, always reminding them to study, to work hard, to keep a journal, to pray, and to exercise self-discipline. What particularly displeased him was the knowledge that none of the boys seemed destined for distinction. None displayed the unique talents of an Adams, and that delinquency offended his sense of family pride. Although his oldest and youngest sons managed to graduate from Harvard, his middle son, John II, was expelled in 1823 for participating in a student riot and nothing his father could say or do convinced the school's authorities to reverse their decision to dismiss the young man.

If Abigail was a calamity as a mother, John Quincy Adams was a disaster as a father—and as a husband.

Fortunately for his own mental well-being he could bury himself in his duties as secretary of state when the situation at home threatened to overwhelm him. And in 1824 he also started thinking seriously about running for president.

As the administration of James Monroe waned, the talk in the capital and among politicians around the country centered on the approaching presidential election. At least three members of the cabinet were invariably mentioned: William H. Crawford, John C. Calhoun, and John Quincy Adams. Crawford, the secretary of the treasury, had been working toward that end and organizing supporters for the past ten years or more. He graciously and perhaps foolishly stepped aside in 1816 and allowed the nomination for the office to go to his rival, James Monroe. He assumed that the president would return the favor and designate him as successor. But Monroe had no such intention and preferred to remain neutral. Calhoun, the very capable secretary of war whom even Adams admired, believed he had strong southern support and only needed Pennsylvania as an anchor in the north. As for John Quincy Adams, he was an automatic candidate by virtue of his office, following in the footsteps of the three previous presidents, Jefferson, Madison, and Monroe, each of whom had served as secretary of state over the last twenty-four years. In fact Adams had received one electoral vote for president in the election of 1820 when Monroe was almost unanimously reelected. Some said that William Plumer of New Hampshire voted for Adams in order to preserve George Washington's record as the only man to be unanimously elected chief executive. Actually, Plumer voted for Adams because he regarded him as eminently qualified to hold the office.

On May 8, 1824, John McLean, the postmaster general, visited the secretary and asked for his opinion on internal improvements, which Adams wholeheartedly supported since he believed the federal government should be an active participant in stimulating the building of bridges, roads, canals, and other forms of transportation. But McLean's obvious intent was to publicize Adams's views on leading issues as a prelude to seeking his nomination. But the very idea of risking defeat in the contest troubled the secretary. "When I consider that to me alone, of all the candidates before the nation, failure of success would be equivalent to a vote of censure by the nation upon my past services, I cannot dissemble to myself that I have more at stake upon the result than any other individual in the Union."

The thought of failure made him shudder. But he realized that if he were able to bear success, "I must be tempered to endure defeat." Anyone who wishes to occupy such an important seat of government, he continued, must "possess resources of a power to serve her even against her own will."

As a candidate, however, Adams had one enormous defect. He did nothing to "excite attention" or gain important friendships, said Associate Supreme Court Justice Joseph Story. "He is retiring and unobtrusive, studious, cool and reflecting." In short he exuded the air of a scholar, not a leader.

Adams himself knew his limitations. "I well know that I never was and never shall be what is commonly termed a popular man." Unfortunately, "I have not the pliability to reform it."

Two other candidates also loomed large in 1824. One was Henry Clay, Speaker of the House, whose ambition for the high office only grew stronger with the passing years. A beloved Speaker in the lower chamber, a gregarious, witty, and charming individual, he would easily win election if no candidate had a majority of electoral votes and the contest went to the House of Representatives for a decision. And with the number of candidates increasing monthly, the likelihood of a House election became more and more certain.

The other candidate, General Andrew Jackson, was at first discounted as utterly without the necessary credentials for the presidency. True, his education was meager, and his record of public service in any legislative body sparse; still, he was the most popular man in the nation by virtue of his spectacular victory over the British at New Orleans during the War of 1812. After that he seized Florida, making it possible for JQA to negotiate the nation's expansion to the Pacific. Then, suddenly, he found political leaders around the country attracted to his possible candidacy. To extend his visibility, the legislature of his home state of Tennessee subsequently elected him to the United States Senate so that other politicians could get a closer look at him and he could embellish his record of public service. Thus, as it finally developed, the contest of 1824 involved two southerners (Calhoun and Crawford), two westerners (Jackson and Clay), but only one northerner, John Quincy Adams.

Since candidates did not actively campaign at this time, most of these individuals had managers, ranging from the politically astute, such as Senator Martin Van Buren of New York (referred to frequently as the Little Magician) who supported William H. Crawford, to Senator John H. Eaton of Tennessee, the ward and close friend of General Jackson. For his part Adams refused to electioneer or actively seek the support of other politicians. Yet he desperately wanted the presidency, if for no other reason than that it would prove to his father that he was a worthy son. However, he soon discovered, like so many men who succeeded him, that if he really wanted the prize he had to reach for it. His halting efforts took several forms.

To start he sought to rid himself of possible rivals, suggesting to Monroe at various times that Jackson, Clay, and Calhoun be sent off on foreign missions in either Latin America or Europe. When that ploy failed he tried another: enticing Jackson into a political alliance. He convinced his reluctant wife to give an enormous ball to honor the general on the approaching ninth anniversary of the victory over the British by informing her that he wanted Jackson on his ticket as vice president. Privately he commented that if Jackson accepted such an alliance it would "afford an easy and dignified retirement to his old age." (Actually Adams and Jackson were both born the same year; Jackson was four months older.) Louisa dutifully gave one of the most splendid balls in anyone's memory. Over a thousand people attended and Jackson obliged his host by giving a toast that seemed to signal his acceptance of an Adams-Jackson ticket. Unfortunately for JQA it was the furthest thought from Jackson's mind.

Next Adams advertised his competence in the public prints. He provided notes and information to editors who prepared glowing accounts of his diplomatic successes or elaborate defenses of his alleged errors of judgment or mistakes of policy as congressman, diplomat, and secretary of state. In many instances he was the "anonymous" author of these editorials. There were a number of newspaper attacks, all of which he leveled with such skill in marshaling evidence in his defense that it took a brave individual to challenge his veracity in print. One example involved accusations by Jonathan Russell, who tried to help Clay's campaign by charging that Adams had groveled before the British at Ghent over control of the Mississippi and the fisheries. The secretary personally responded in a book-length refutation, proving Russell had used doctored documents in presenting his case. Adams made a shambles of the arguments against him and in the process demolished Russell's career.

In addition to everything else, Adams began socializing at every opportunity, hardly missing an event in Washington that could advance his candidacy. He assured the few Federalists still active in politics that he bore no animosity toward them nor would he necessarily deny them positions in government because of their opinions. As for Republicans he had long since demonstrated his value and loyalty, even though he liked to think he rose above parties.

Then a series of events occurred that dramatically altered the course of the election. First, William H. Crawford suffered a debilitating stroke that left him partially paralyzed, speechless, and almost sightless. Still, his supporters, led by Van Buren, insisted that the traditional form of nominating the Republican presidential candidate be followed, namely the convocation of a caucus of congressional Republicans. Since there were more Crawford Republicans in the two houses, their insistence on following this route was vehemently opposed by the supporters of the other candidates. "King Caucus is dead," they shouted; it is undemocratic. Actually, the caucus allowed a small group of men in Congress to decide who would win the White House since the Republican party's nominee would automatically win. The Federalist party was moribund, and although it continued to function in some northern states, especially in New England, it did not nominate a candidate for the 1824 election.

Despite the derisive complaints Van Buren summoned the congressional caucus to meet on February 14, 1824, in the chamber of the House of Representatives. But only sixty-six members attended. The other congressmen stayed away in protest. Dismissing cries from the galleries that the meeting adjourn, Van Buren pressed on to a final vote. To no one's surprise, Crawford won the nomination with sixty-two votes, Adams received two, and Jackson and Nathaniel Macon of North Carolina had one apiece. The caucus then named Albert Gallatin as vice president. But the nomination did Crawford more harm than good. It gave the other candidates the opportunity to publicly denounce the caucus as an affront to every intelligent voter in America.

Hard on the heels of this event came the results of the Pennsylvania convention on which John C. Calhoun based his hope for northern support. Without Pennsylvania, Calhoun was simply another southern candidate without the slightest chance of winning in the general election. To his chagrin Pennsylvania deserted him. At the convention held on March 4 the delegates chose Andrew Jackson for president and Calhoun for vice president, an action later imitated by New Jersey, Maryland, and North and South Carolina. Bowing to the inevitable, Calhoun withdrew as a presidential candidate.

As for Adams's nomination he had many partisans in New England who held rallies on his behalf. One such meeting of supporters took place in Faneuil Hall in Boston on February 15, 1824, at which he was formally named as their candidate. The Republican members of the Massachusetts legislature followed suit on June 10, as did the other New England states shortly thereafter. A campaign biography was quickly assembled by a Philadelphia editor, Joseph E. Hall, and Congressman Joseph Hopkinson urged Adams to help organize a nationwide campaign. But Adams steadfastly refused. "I will take not one step to advance or promote pretensions to the Presidency," he replied. He obviously wanted the presidency and would do whatever he could to obtain the office but it had to be done discreetly and aboveboard. He would compose oceans of words in self-defense for some previous action of his, but he would not assist any organized effort that might give the appearance of soliciting votes. It never seemed to occur to him that his behavior frequently contradicted his intentions.

Since the state legislatures in six of the twenty-four states in the Union chose their presidential electors, rather than the voters themselves, political brokers in those states lobbied intensively for their candidates. In New York the friends of Adams approached the Clay supporters with a proposal that they split the electoral votes between them. But the Clay men rejected the offer and they did so with their candidate's approval. "If I am elected," the Speaker boasted, "I shall enter upon the office without one solitary promise or pledge to any man to redeem."

It was an unfortunate decision. With all the skullduggery that took place before, during, and even after the New York legislature chose its electors the final result as transmitted to Washington gave twenty-six votes for Adams, one for Jackson, five for Crawford, and only four for Clay. A "fouler" and more "dishonorable piece of management could not in my estimation be adopted," fumed one Clay supporter.

When the popular and electoral votes were tabulated from around the country Jackson had a plurality of 152,901 popular and 99 electoral votes, Adams had 114,023 popular and 84 electoral votes, Crawford garnered 46,979 popular and 41 electoral votes, and Clay came last with 47,217 popular and 37 electoral votes.

New England and most of New York voted for Adams. Jackson won Tennessee, Pennsylvania, New Jersey, Indiana, and most of Maryland and the South. Crawford took Virginia and his home state of Georgia. Clay captured Kentucky, Ohio, and Missouri.

John C. Calhoun easily won the vice presidency, receiving 182 electoral votes to 30 for Nathan Sanford, 24 for Nathaniel Macon, 13 for Jackson, 9 for Van Buren, and 2 for Clay.

Since no candidate had a majority of electoral votes as required by the Constitution, the election automatically went to the House of Representatives for the final selection. And since the 12th Amendment limited the number before the House to the top three, that automatically excluded Clay. Ironically, as the most powerful individual in the House, he would have the most influence in deciding the next president. "It is in fact very much in Clay's power to make the President," wrote Representative William Plumer of New Hampshire. "If he says Jackson, the nine Western states are united at once for him—If he says Adams, two or three Western states fall off—& Jackson must fail."

The skullduggery of New York politics now shifted to Washington. As Congress reassembled, the managers of the three surviving candidates descended on Clay, urging him to support their man.

"My dear Sir," purred one of Jackson's friends, "all our dependence is on you; don't disappoint us; you know our partiality was for you next to the Hero; and how much we want a western President." Next came a Crawford supporter. "The hopes of the Republican party are concentrated on you. For God's sake preserve it—If you had been returned instead of Mr. Crawford every man of us would have supported you to the last hour. We consider him & you as the only genuine Republican candidates." Even the Adams allies came crawling to Clay "with tears in their eyes. Sir Mr. Adams has always had the greatest respect for you, & admiration for your talents— There is no station to which they are not equal—Most undoubtedly you were the second choice of New England. And I pray you to consider seriously whether the public good & your own future interests do not point most distinctly to the choice which you ought to make."

Your own future interests. That was Clay's concern too. And between the three candidates there really was no contest. Two were absolutely impossible as far as he was concerned. Crawford was physically incapable of assuming the presidency, and Jackson was nothing more than a "military chieftain." "I cannot believe," the Speaker wrote, "that killing 2,500 Englishmen at N. Orleans qualifies for the various, difficult and complicated duties of the Chief Magistracy." No, it had to be Adams, and even though he thoroughly disliked the man he had to admit that the secretary was the best qualified for the job. Still, the Speaker had no intention of supporting Adams until he had spoken with him and received assurances about what might be expected in case of his election. Was it really in the Kentuckian's "own future interests" to throw his weight behind the secretary of state? He needed to hear firsthand from Adams about his intentions. So he dispatched his Kentucky colleague and messmate, Robert Letcher, to pay a call on the secretary and ask him what his "sentiments towards Clay were."

The interview took place on December 12, 1824, and Adams replied to the question by assuring Letcher that he harbored no hostility against the Speaker. But he was no fool. He knew exactly what Letcher was implying, namely "that Clay would willingly support me if he could thereby serve himself, and . . . if Clay's friends could *know* that he would have a prominent share in the Administration, that might induce them to vote for me, even in the face of instructions."

Even in the face of instructions. What Adams was referring to were the likely instructions to be sent by the Kentucky legislature to its congressional delegation instructing them to cast the state's vote for the western candidate in the House election. That obviously meant Jackson.

Not much later, Adams, still pretending he was not electioneering in any way, gave a dinner party to which most of the leading figures in the campaign were invited. Then, on Sunday, January 9, 1825, Clay sent a note to Adams asking if he could stop by for a visit that very evening.

At six o'clock Clay arrived. Together the two men talked for three hours, conversing about the past and the future. "The time has come for me to make a decision," said Clay. At that he asked the secretary "to satisfy him with regard to some principles of great public importance, but without any personal considerations for myself."

Adams recorded the conversation in his journal. But at the point where Clay asked for a declaration of "some principles of great public importance," Adams abruptly ended his narrative. Exactly what he said in response to the request is unknown. They did talk about "expectations for the future," or so Adams informed a friend several days later. Was there a quid pro quo arrangement of any kind? No one knows for certain. But most probably they agreed to implement Clay's American System, a program that called for protective tariff legislation, advancement of public works, and the support of the Second National Bank of the United States, all of which Adams could easily endorse. When the interview ended, Clay informed Adams that he "had no hesitation in saying that his preference would be for me."

Two days later the Kentucky legislature passed resolutions stating that it was "the wish of the people of Kentucky" that the western candidate receive the state's vote. In open defiance, and at the behest of Clay, the Kentucky delegation announced on January 24 its decision to cast its vote for Adams. There was an immediate uproar. "We are in commotion," declared Robert Y. Hayne of South Carolina, "about the monstrous union between Clay & Adams." Martin Van Buren was thunderstruck. If you do this, he told a Kentucky representative, "you sign Mr. Clay's political death warrant. He will never become President be your motives as pure as you claim them to be."

It was immediately assumed that the two men had made a deal, a bargain, and a "corrupt bargain" at that, in which Clay would supply Adams with enough votes to be elected president and Adams in return would appoint Clay as his secretary of state, the recognized stepping stone to the presidency. "All the waters of the sweet Heavens cannot remove the iota of corruption," cried Representative Louis McLane.

But what did they expect Clay to do? "That I should vote for Mr. Crawford? I cannot. For Gen. Jackson? I will not. I shall pursue the course which my conscience dictates, regardless of all imputations and all consequences."

In the midst of this political maneuvering, Adams himself engaged in several other "bargains." He was approached by Representative John Scott, who, as the single representative from Missouri, would cast that state's vote. Scott presented Adams with a list of printers whom he wanted appointed as printers of the laws of Missouri. Adams assured him they would receive the coveted assignments. Scott actually "voted for Adams, the way Clay told him to do" and Adams, as president, later reappointed Scott's brother to the Arkansas bench in violation of territorial law. The brother had killed a colleague in a duel, and the law forbade any participant in a duel to hold public office. However, the Senate refused to confirm the reappointment.

Adams also had an agreement with Representative Henry R. Warfield, a man whose vote might break a tie in the Maryland delegation. Two days before the election was scheduled to take place in the House, Warfield visited the secretary and expressed the fear that, if elected, President Adams would exclude Federalists from office. Daniel Webster voiced the same concern. The Federalist party no longer existed as a national organization, leaving the political field completely to the Republican party, but within certain states like Maryland and in New England, Federalists continued to hold office and even send representatives to Congress. Both Warfield and

Webster, among others, wanted assurances that Adams would not remove those Federalists already in office or exclude them from future appointments.

Not to worry. The affable Adams assured them both "that I never would be at the head of any Administration of proscription to any party—political or geographical."

Warfield expressed his satisfaction with the disavowal and then informed Adams that the "Patroon," Stephen Van Rensselaer of New York, would also appreciate receiving similar assurances and that he would advise the Patroon to visit the secretary and obtain confirmation firsthand. As it turned out the votes of both Warfield and the Patroon were pivotal.

The House election was held on a snowy Wednesday, February 9, 1825. When Representative Van Rensselaer arrived he was hustled into Henry Clay's private office, where the Speaker and Daniel Webster urged him to repudiate his promise to Van Buren not to vote for Adams on the first ballot. The New York vote was split and the Magician hoped to keep it that way for several fruitless rounds of balloting and then step in and swing the state to Crawford. So he got Van Rensselaer to give him his word not to vote for Adams during the initial round. Knowing that the Patroon was an intensely religious man, Van Buren believed the promise would not be broken.

Poor Van Rensselaer. He staggered out of Clay's office, visibly upset and muttering about how "the vote of New York . . . depended upon him" and "if he gave it to A. he could be elected most probably on the first ballot."

Shortly after noon the balloting began. Each state had one vote determined by the delegation, with a majority of thirteen states needed for election. The votes of Delaware, Illinois, Mississippi, and Missouri were cast by a single representative. Adams expected to take all six New England votes plus Kentucky, Ohio, Missouri, and possibly Louisiana, thanks to the influence of Henry Clay. As it turned out, courtesy of Webster and Warfield, Maryland cast its vote for Adams, despite the fact that Jackson had won most of its electoral vote in the fall election. Illinois also went to Adams through the action of Representative Daniel Cook, who may or may not have been bribed. When Cook lost his next election to Congress, Adams graciously appointed him to a confidential "diplomatic junket to Cuba" paid for out of Secret Service funds.

As the ballot box neared him, Van Rensselaer lowered his head to his desk and prayed for divine guidance. Then, as he raised himself to an upright position he spotted a ballot lying on the floor with the name of John Quincy Adams. A man of his faith immediately saw it as an answer to his prayer and with "great excitement" picked up the ballot and thrust it into the ballot box. According to Van Buren, that single vote broke the New York tie and elected Adams as the sixth president of the United States. (Actually, New York's vote was Adams eighteen, Crawford fourteen, and Jackson two.) On the first ballot thirteen states had voted for Adams, seven for Jackson, and four for Crawford. "Partisan friends of Adams burst into applause" when the result was announced. "The cards were stacked," sneered John Randolph of Roanoke.

A delegation was appointed to bring the result directly to Adams.

"May the blessing of God rest upon the event of this day!" the fifty-eight-year-old president-elect responded to Alexander H. Everett when he received the news. Then he quickly wrote a brief note to his father with the comment, "I can only offer you my congratulations and ask your blessings and prayers." To which the aged father responded by invoking "the blessing of God Almighty" on his son.

President Monroe gave a levee to honor the president-elect, and it attracted many guests. "There is our '*Clay President*,'" mocked one man as he pointed to Adams, "and he will be moulded at that man's will and pleasure as easily as clay in a potter's hands." Several days later Clay asked to speak to Adams and they held a long conversation at the end of which the president-elect invited the Kentuckian to join his cabinet as secretary of state.

Clay hesitated. Already there had been talk of a "corrupt bargain" and his acceptance was certain to look like the consummation of a previous "arrangement," but he desperately wanted the post. Finally he convinced himself that he could not vote for the man and encourage others to do so and then refuse to serve under him. Another consideration was the fact that as the head of the State Department he could advance certain causes he held dear, such as Latin American independence. So, after a week of deliberation, he accepted.

It was the worst mistake of his life.

The friends of Jackson erupted when they heard the news. The general himself put it very simply: "Clay voted for Adams and made him President and Adams made Clay secretary of state. Is this not proof as strong as holy writ of the understanding and corrupt coalition between them." The winner of both the popular and the electoral votes then resigned his Senate seat and headed home for Tennessee determined to strike back by running for the presidency against Adams in 1828. "So you see," he raged, "the Judas of the West has closed the contract and will receive the thirty pieces of silver. His end will be the same. Was there ever witnessed such a bare faced corruption in any country before?" The people had been cheated of their right to select their own president, he ranted. "Corrupt" politicians in Washington had stolen it and must be hurled from office at the first opportunity.

And on that note the presidential election of 1828 began at once.

6

"The Perilous Experiment"

For President Adams the selection of Henry Clay to head the cabinet was both swift and expected. No other choice was possible. No other choice made any sense. And no other choice was even considered. Fundamentally they were in ideological agreement, but most important of all, both were committed to advancing the strength and power of the Union. Both were nationalists who had a vision about the future possibilities of the country and how they could be attained. Earlier Adams had informed Monroe and the secretary of the navy, Samuel Southard, of his decision to appoint Clay. "I consider it due to his talents and services," he told Monroe, "and to the Western section of the Union, whence he comes, and to the confidence in me manifested by their delegations." Years later he agreed that he had made one of the worst mistakes of his life.

On inauguration day, March 4, 1825, Adams recorded his thoughts on this momentous occasion. "After two successive sleepless nights," he wrote, "I entered upon this day with a supplication to Heaven, first, for my country; secondly, for myself and for those connected with my good name and fortunes, that the last results of its events may be auspicious and blessed." Then, accompanied by companies of militiamen, he arrived at the Capitol and was inaugurated in the presence of Monroe, Vice President Calhoun, and many of his rivals and friends. In his address he spoke about his belief that "the will of the people is the source and the happiness of the people the end of all legitimate government upon earth." He also described how the country had grown into a "confederated representative democracy," a term not used publicly by any previous president. When he concluded his remarks he took the oath of office from Chief Justice John Marshall.

Three days later the Senate confirmed his nominations to the various cabinet posts. He had wanted to retain Monroe's cabinet as much as possible (as though his administration in personnel and goals would be a continuation of Monroe's), but Crawford refused the invitation and was replaced by Richard Rush, former minister to Great Britain. The president also thought of asking Jackson to take over the War Department, but on sober, second thought he realized it would be a mistake. So he invited James Barbour, former governor of Virginia, to assume the office, and his invitation was accepted. Both William Wirt, the attorney general, and Samuel Southard, secretary of the navy, agreed to remain at their posts, which completed the cabinet. Adams also kept John McLean as postmaster general (not yet a cabinet position), despite the fact that McLean himself was regarded as a partisan of Jackson and Calhoun. The Senate unanimously confirmed his selections—except, of course, Henry Clay. The Kentuckian was finally approved but by the embarrassing vote of twenty-seven to fourteen.

Adams redeemed his promise to the Federalists by appointing the aged Rufus King, who had unsuccessfully run for the presidency on the Federalist ticket in 1816, as minister to Great Britain, replacing Richard Rush. He also rewarded Louisiana, which gave him its vote in the House election even though its electoral vote had gone to Jackson the previous fall, by appointing its senator, James Brown, minister to France. Had Adams used the patronage available to him in coalescing friends and independents into a workable coalition he might have had a more successful administration. But that was not his style. In general his appointments reveal a most inept politician.

For example, throughout his entire administration the rank and file of the civil service remained as it had been. Adams merely filled vacancies when they occurred, and invariably he enlisted qualified individuals, not necessarily those who could advance his strength in Congress. As a matter of fact he only removed twelve persons from office during his entire tenure. Even when it became increasingly obvious that Postmaster General McLean was using the extensive patronage of his office to help the opposition, Adams still refused to remove him because he was an excellent administrator. Clearly the president was off to a very bad start.

But if devotion to duty and the responsibilities of his office meant anything, Adams set an excellent example for other members of the government. As was his custom he rose at five or six o'clock, depending on the time of year, which was usually one and a half to two hours before sunrise. He then walked for four miles, returning to the White House about the time the sun rose. Once back in the mansion he would light the fire, read three chapters of the Bible with commentaries, and then survey the newspapers and public documents until it was time for breakfast, which usually came at nine. At ten he met with individual cabinet members, followed by a succession of congressmen and other visitors, all of which might last until four or five in the afternoon. If possible he took a three- or four-mile walk before dinner, unless weather permitted a swim in the Potomac. He dined from five to six-thirty, after which he talked with Louisa or played billiards or signed documents and wrote up his diary. He usually retired between eleven and twelve.

His public swimming scandalized many, especially on June 13, 1825, when he was forced to jump overboard from a sinking rowboat. Fully clothed with a long-sleeved shirt and baggy pants, he soon found himself "struggling for life and gasping for breath." He managed to gain the shore where he stripped while a servant, who had gone with him, searched for help. Five hours later they returned to the White House but already a rumor had circulated that he had drowned.

Within days of taking office Adams realized that a very strong opposition was building against his administration. The Senate rejected a treaty with Colombia that he had negotiated as secretary of state for the suppression of the slave trade, and the friends of Jackson had already begun publicly denouncing him and Clay as having stolen the election. The political signs were beginning to show that the nation was moving away from the so-called Era of Good Feelings in which one party, the Republican party, held complete sway in national affairs. But, as Adams would soon point out in his first annual message to Congress in December 1825, he needed overwhelming support in Congress to achieve the goals he sought for the benefit of the American people. A strong opposition could jeopardize it completely.

He spent considerable time working on his message, and by November 22 he had completed a preliminary draft that he read to his cabinet. In it he proposed a series of internal improvements and the creation of a Department of the Interior to handle the mounting domestic problems in the country. The cabinet thought his ideas hopelessly unrealistic and sure to fail, but such criticisms only spurred the proud New Englander to push ahead. Sooner or later, he insisted, his ideas for the country's future would have to be articulated. And nothing, not politics nor the practicality of his proposals, would hold him back. "The perilous experiment is to be made," he jotted down in his diary that evening. "Let me make it with full deliberation, and be prepared for the consequences."

Attorney General William Wirt had been out of town when the message was read to the cabinet and upon his return he asked to see the document. Adams read it to him, and as he proceeded through page after page, Wirt's face clearly registered his displeasure.

"It is excessively bold," Wirt declared when the president concluded his reading. "There is not a line in it which I do not approve." Still, it will "give strong hold to the party . . . who represent you as grasping for power." States' righters will be outraged at its assertion of governmental power and it will be "a great source of clamor."

John Quincy Adams was hardly the man to be intimidated by the forebodings of others. He believed in what he had written. His purpose, he later wrote, was "the ultimate improvement and exaltation of the nature of man and his condition on earth." Fully determined now to proceed, he sent the message down to Congress on December 5 to be read by a clerk.

And it nearly blew the dome off the Capitol building. It began with a small explosion. He mentioned that a congress of South American nations would meet in Panama to discuss problems of mutual concern. The United States had been invited to attend and the invitation had been accepted. Ministers would be named shortly and the Senate would be asked to confirm them. That information in and of itself triggered protest. It was bad enough to get involved with foreign countries discussing matters that did not concern the United States, but the idea of sitting at a conference with delegates from Caribbean islands, some of whom were former slaves, outraged southerners.

Adams then spoke of U.S. relations with European nations, the improved condition of finances, the state of the nation's defenses and the needs of the army and navy, the relations with Indian tribes, a national bankruptcy law, and the desirability of a more efficient patent law so that the rights of inventors would be protected—all of which were innocuous enough. Then came the main explosion. "The great object of the institution of civil government is the improvement of the condition of those who are parties to the social compact, and no government, in whatever form constituted, can accomplish the lawful ends of its institution but in proportion as it improves the condition of those over whom it is established."

Could there be any clearer assertion of the doctrine of affirmative government?

The particulars followed. He proposed the building of an extensive system of roads and canals, bridges, and highways. Not content with that controversial request he went on to say that among the first, "perhaps the very first, instrument for the improvement of the condition of men is knowledge." To that end he recommended the founding of a national university and a naval academy similar to West Point in order "to prepare for all the emergencies of peace and war." He further recommended the "erection of an astronomical observatory," with provision for the support of an astronomer "to be in constant attendance of observation upon the phenomena of the heavens, and for the periodical publication of his observations." European governments maintained 130 of these "lighthouses of the skies" while the United States had not one. It was time for this country to follow their example.

He also wanted the establishment of a uniform standard of weights and measures. And he suggested that the United States imitate Great Britain and France, which had already begun "profound, laborious and expensive researches into the figure of the earth and the comparative length of the pendulum vibrating seconds in various latitudes from the equator to the pole. . . . It would be honorable to our country . . . [if similar] experiments should be countenanced by the patronage of our Government."

Some Congressmen surely thought the president had lost his mind. The proposals were preposterous, they exclaimed. Think of the cost alone, to say nothing of the violations of the Constitution that these recommendations entailed.

But the message got worse. The interior of the nation had not been fully explored nor the coastline and many places along the Pacific Ocean "have been barely visited by our public ships." He therefore recommended the "exploration of the whole northwest coast of this continent" and the creation of an additional executive Department of the Interior.

> The spirit of improvement is abroad upon the earth. It stimulates hearts and sharpens the faculties not of our fellow-citizens alone, but of the nations of Europe and of their rulers. While dwelling with pleasing satisfaction upon the superior excellence of our political institutions, let us not be unmindful that liberty is power; that the nation blessed with the largest portion of liberty must in proportion to its members be the most powerful nation upon earth. While foreign nations less blessed with that freedom which is power than ourselves are advancing with gigantic strides in the career of public improvement were we to slumber in indolence or fold up our arms and proclaim to the world that we are palsied by the will of our constituents, would it not be to cast away the bounties of Providence and doom ourselves to perpetual inferiority?

Palsied by the will of our constituents! That phrase alone convulsed the opposition. Who did he think the members of Congress represented? It was further proof that the administration had come to power through corruption and the total disregard of the wishes of the American people.

But here was a bold, courageous, and statesmanlike assertion of what the national government could do to advance the economic, intellectual, and cultural well-being of the nation. He presented to Congress a program of breathtaking scope. He offered a vision of what could be achieved to increase the happiness of the people, and he tried to point out the responsibilities of a country blessed with a freely elected government that no other nation in the world enjoyed. Henry Clay had long insisted that the central government must stimulate and improve the economy by providing internal improvements, a sound banking system, and protection for manufacturers so they could compete in world markets. His American System, as Clay called it, was firmly anchored in Hamilton's economic program, which was the basis of the old Federalist party. But states' righters only saw the message as one gigantic grab for power and they vowed to extinguish every one of Adams's "lighthouses of the skies," as they derisively called his program.

Small wonder that the entire cabinet opposed presenting it at this time. It was sure to polarize the several factions that composed the developing opposition and perhaps weld them into a single party. The followers of Crawford, Calhoun, and Jackson each had reasons to hate what Adams had put forward. The friends of Crawford, like Van Buren, were strict constructionists and worried about what the expansion of governmental authority would mean in terms of individual liberty. Said one: "The message of the President seems to claim all the power to the federal Government." As for the Calhoun men they were deathly opposed to tariffs or anything suggesting protection for manufacturers. They argued that the administration would gratify the demands of northerners (especially those in New England) over those of southerners. And the Jacksonians, of course, regarded the entire administration as illegitimate, its proposals unworthy of serious consideration. "When I view the splendor & magnificence of the government," wrote Jackson, "embraced in the recommendation of the late message, with the powers enumerated, which may be rightfully exercised by congress to lead to this magnificence, together with the declaration that it would be criminal for the agents of our government to be palsied by the will of their constituents, I shudder for the consequence—if not checked by the voice of the people, it must end in consolidation, & then in despotism."

As for the Panama Congress, the opposition abominated the idea. "The moment we engage in confederations or alliances with any nation," Jackson wrote, "we may from that time date the downfall of our republic." The Panama Mission was judged an unwarranted intrusion into the treaty-making power of the Senate and a barefaced "attempt to destroy the constitutional checks of our government, and to reduce it to a despotism . . . to register the *edicts* of the President."

Van Buren and the other Crawford strict constructionists could not agree more. To them the Panama Congress was a violent departure from the established foreign policy set down by George Washington in his Farewell Address. The very least the president should do "is obtain the consent of the people to the expediency of this measure . . . at least by their representatives in congress."

Concerned about this Panama Mission, Senator Martin Van Buren visited Vice President Calhoun to learn what the Jacksonians felt about the question. He presumed that Calhoun and Jackson were already allied, and although that was not true at the moment it soon would be. In any event he was pleased to hear that the vice president also opposed the conference and the two men ended their conversation with an implicit understanding of what they would do and where they were headed.

Adams first suspected "a union of Crawford, Calhoun and Jackson partisans" when the House called for some important papers relative to the Panama question, but he was certain of it when the Senate began debating the nominations of ministers to the conference sent down on December 26, 1825. He proposed Richard C. Anderson of Kentucky and John Sergeant of Pennsylvania as ministers and William R. Rochester of New York as secretary. The Senate opposition immediately organized and prepared to filibuster the nominations to death; and one of its members, John Randolph of Roanoke, the senator from Virginia, led off by denouncing the mission as a "Kentucky cuckoo's egg, laid in a Spanish-American nest."

The reference to Kentucky was clear to everyone. Secretary of State Henry Clay was the mastermind behind the Panama Mission. As early as the previous spring he had had a series of discussions with the ministers of Mexico and Colombia, Pablo Obregón and José María Salazar, in which they asked his help in winning U.S.

attendance at the Panama Congress. They did not wish to issue an invitation unless they had prior knowledge that it would be accepted. Clay succeeded in gaining the administration's approval, despite Adams's initial hesitation. By attending what would be the first Pan-American Conference, an idea originally formulated by Simón Bolívar, the United States could inaugurate a "Good Neighborhood Policy," as Clay called it, especially with those Latin American countries that had just attained their independence.

Naturally Senator Van Buren played a leading role in organizing the opposition in the upper house, while Thomas Hart Benton of Missouri, Robert Y. Hayne of South Carolina, John M. Berrien of Georgia, and John Holmes of Maine carried out the main lines of attack. Hayne voiced Southern fears that the mission would discuss the suppression of the slave trade. "With nothing connected with slavery can we consent to treat with other nations," he thundered.

Van Buren himself followed and condemned the manner in which Adams had acted toward the Senate. The president's slow response in sending down needed documents so that the legislators could evaluate the mission demonstrated, he said, a high-handed and reckless contempt of the Constitution and the Congress. Moreover, he feared that the Panama delegates would legislate some action or other, thereby undercutting the power of the U.S. Congress. Benton, Berrien, and Holmes all concentrated on the constitutional issue but it remained for Senator Randolph to add verbal pyrotechnics to the debate. In a six-hour harangue he launched a personal attack on Clay and Adams and said that their coalition reminded him of "Blifill and Black George . . . the puritan and the black-leg," two disreputable characters in *Tom Jones*, a popular novel of the day by Henry Fielding. Clay responded by challenging Randolph to a duel but fortunately neither man was injured.

It infuriated Adams that the presiding officer of the Senate, Vice President Calhoun, did not put a stop to this verbal abuse the instant it started. The vice president permitted Randolph "in speeches of ten hours long to drink himself drunk with bottled porter, and, in raving balderdash . . . to revile the absent and the present, the living and the dead," recorded the president. "This was tolerated by Calhoun because Randolph's ribaldry was all pointed against the Administration, especially against Mr. Clay and me, and because he was afraid of Randolph."

Such was the tone of the debate, which dragged on for months. Finally in March 1826 the administration forces managed to defeat a resolution declaring the conference inexpedient and won confirmation of the two ministers and secretary by a vote of twenty-seven to seventeen.

But the opposition was not done. In the House the members tried to express their disapproval by holding up the appropriation for the mission. They succeeded in delaying authorization until early May when, by the vote of 134 to 60, the money was finally appropriated. At first it seemed like a clear-cut victory for the administration. Unfortunately, one minister died en route to Panama and, because of the delay, the other envoy did not arrive at the conference until after it had adjourned.

By this time the opposition had come to the conclusion that the only way to rid the country of this "cursed union of 'puritan and black-leg'" was to unite behind Andrew Jackson and elect him president in 1828. "*He* is the only man that can break down this union," wrote one strict constructionist, and restore legitimate government. His election will achieve "the substantial reorganization of the old Republican party."

Thus, within a matter of months, the friends of Crawford and Calhoun united with those of Jackson to form the Democratic Republican party or simply the Democratic party, advocating Jeffersonian principles of limited government and strict economy. Their new party, wrote Van Buren to Thomas Ritchie, leader of the Crawford forces in Virginia and the editor of the *Richmond Enquirer*, would bring about a union of "Southern planters and plain republicans of the North." On the other hand, the administration party— that is, the coalition of Adams and Clay and other ardent nationalists who favored the president's program and viewed government as a necessary instrument to advance the interests of the American people—called themselves National Republicans.

As for the other proposals in Adams's breathtaking vision, the national university was the easiest for the Democrats to defeat. For them the argument first stated by President Madison about its lack of constitutional authority was sufficient to squelch any hope for such an institution. And the fact that George Washington University had been chartered in the District of Columbia in 1821 gave the opposition sufficient reason for ignoring the idea. It simply sank without a trace.

The naval academy scheme had a better reception. It was debated in Congress and legislation actually came up for a vote. The Senate consented, twenty-four to twenty-two, but the House turned it down, eighty-six to seventy-eight, as too costly. It was estimated that the government would have to pay nine professors the princely sum of $7,000!

The "lighthouses of the skies" idea was simply laughed at by many congressmen and a uniform standard of weights and measures proposal ignored. An avid supporter of scientific investigation and observation, Adams was deeply disappointed by the lack of any legislation to improve "those parts of knowledge which lie beyond the reach of individual acquisition."

As one proposal after another failed to gain approval for the country's intellectual and scientific pursuits, Adams privately renewed his own scientific interests, particularly the study of botany. Consular officials, naval officers, and anyone having access to interesting and unusual species of animals, plants, and seeds were asked to inform him of them or arrange their importation.

Even the proposal for a coastal survey of the eastern seaboard—it was remembered that during the War of 1812 the British had better navigational information than Americans about the coastline—failed to generate the needed legislation. However, local projects such as the survey of the Charleston, Savannah, and Baltimore harbors or the route of the proposed Chesapeake and Ohio Canal had an easier time of gaining congressional support since local constituencies were involved and winning votes for them cut across party lines.

Moreover, during Adams's administration the National Road that began at Cumberland, Maryland, was extended from Wheeling, Virginia, to Zanesville, Ohio. Local projects, such as new canals, were opened or their construction begun, including the Cleveland

and Akron Canal, the Dismal Swamp Canal, the Chesapeake and Ohio Canal, and the Louisville and Portland Canal around the falls of the Ohio River. On July 4, 1828, construction of the first passenger railway got under way with the building of the Baltimore and Ohio Railroad, thus opening up a whole new mode of transportation that would ultimately stretch across the United States from coast to coast and bind together citizens of different regions and sections. Of course many of these projects were undertaken by private stock companies but the assistance of the national government, either by outright grants of money or land, provided much of the impetus for the transformation of the country from a purely agricultural to an industrial society.

A bankruptcy bill brought forward in the House and Senate early in 1827 divided the Congress between those who wanted a general law covering everyone and those who favored limiting it to merchants and traders. Strict constructionists insisted that any bankruptcy bill lacked constitutional authorization and would encourage insolvency. Unfortunately sectional economic interests as well as partisan opposition combined to defeat the bill in the Senate, twenty-seven to twenty-one.

On the issue of public lands owned by the federal government, Adams alienated potential supporters throughout the country who favored selling the land to settlers at a cheap price. The Land Act of 1820 lowered the price to $1.25 per acre with minimum purchases fixed at eighty acres. But Senator Thomas Hart Benton of Missouri, who had supported Clay in the election of 1824 but switched to Jackson after the election, advocated a graduated reduction of the price still further and even giving the land away to settlers when it went unsold. He also argued for passage of a preemption law that would allow squatters to have a prior claim to the property over speculators.

Adams adamantly opposed the Benton position. For him public land was a means of paying off the national debt and financing internal improvements. In this way it would benefit all the people, not just settlers. Benton managed to get his bill to the floor of the Senate in 1828 but it went down to defeat, twenty-four to twenty-one, by a combination of National Republicans and several eastern Democrats. But Adams got most of the blame for its defeat and it cost him dearly in Missouri, Illinois, and Indiana.

This hemorrhaging of support became lethal when the administration turned to the troublesome questions of Indian removal and tariff legislation. Even diplomacy failed to provide a needed triumph. All these issues resulted in the steady lowering of the Adams administration into its political grave.

7

Indian Removal

When John Quincy and Louisa with their two younger sons, John II and Charles Francis, finally settled into the White House—the mansion was left in such dreadful condition by the Monroes that they could not take up residence in the building until April 5—they rattled around in an enormous building devoid of running water or plumbing and maintained by a small group of servants, including JQA's personal valet, Antoine Giusta. Congress provided money for household expenses, and Adams purchased a silver service from the Russian minister, Baron von Tuyll, and additional silver plate from William H. Crawford. To provide relaxation he also bought a set of chessmen and a billiard table, cues, and balls. He liked nothing better than a game of billiards in the evening, but afterward he would upbraid himself for wasting his time when there was important work to be done.

The Democrats would later use these purchases to charge him with recklessly spending public money on "royal extravagances." A report of White House expenditures was submitted to a Congressional Committee on Retrenchment in which it said that public funds had been used to outfit the East Room with gambling equipment. Although Adams later corrected this report to show that he had purchased these items out of his own pocket, the Democrats continued to berate him for having such equipment in the executive mansion. An article entitled "The East Room," written anonymously by Senator Benton and published in the *Richmond Enquirer*, attacked the president for spending $25,000 on "gambling furniture" and other unseemly paraphernalia.

General Lafayette visited the family and stayed in the White House during July and August 1825 before returning home after a long nationwide tour. And George Washington Adams, the eldest son, frequently visited. He had completed his education at Harvard and training in the law and had won election to the Massachusetts legislature. A brilliant but erratic and possibly disturbed young man, he made a mess of his father's personal affairs in Boston, which had been entrusted to him, and caused his parents considerable grief. John II tried to assist his father as private secretary but he too gave the president and Louisa many anxious moments on account of his drinking problem. Only the youngest son, Charles Francis, showed signs that he fit the accepted Adams mold. He graduated Harvard at the age of eighteen, studied law with his father for two years, and returned to Boston where he was admitted to the Massachusetts bar in 1829.

The president had great hopes for his three sons. He wanted them to follow careers of public service, just as he and their grandfather had done. So he wrote them every week, directed their work and study habits, and reminded them constantly of what was expected of them. Of the three only Charles Francis responded satisfactorily to his demands, and in time they came to appreciate each other's intellectual strengths. Together they engaged in a regular and rewarding correspondence that gave the old man much pleasure.

For a vacation John Quincy liked to escape to his home in Quincy, Massachusetts, to visit his father and other relatives. He usually spent from August to October at home. There he felt he could renew his sense of purpose and direction. On July 4, 1826, a few weeks before his expected departure for Quincy, he thought a good deal of his father. It was the fiftieth anniversary of the Declaration of Independence. He sat in the Capitol and listened to orators extol the document that Jefferson, Adams's father, and Benjamin Franklin had fashioned. Jefferson and Adams still lived—but barely. On this day both men died, Jefferson muttering, "Is it the Fourth?" and Adams whispering, "Thomas Jefferson still survives." It seemed

miraculous that both men had lived to welcome the fiftieth anniversary of this momentous document.

When John Quincy received word of his father's failing health
and the fact that he might succumb at any moment he sped away to
get home in time. However, at Waterloo, a short distance to Baltimore, he was informed of his father's death. He did not reach Quincy
until July 13, but the funeral had already taken place six days earlier. For John Quincy the loss of his father was a severe emotional
blow. They had been so close and intimate for John Quincy's entire
life. There were many commemorative services that the president
dutifully attended. But not one of the eulogists, not Daniel Webster,
Horace Mann, Edward Everett, or the president of Harvard, could
assuage the pain and sense of loss he endured.

Adams dreaded returning to Washington and the ongoing formation of an opposition that in the fall election of 1826 would witness the further strengthening of the Jackson forces. He learned
that "meetings and counter meetings, committees of correspondence, delegations and addresses" were attempting to incite "the
passions of the people" both for and against the administration. All
of which turned him into a bitter and depressed grumbler and mal-
content. He now detested Andrew Jackson with a vengeance, a man
he once admired and whose military exploits he defended. The
nation seemed intent on placing this "illiterate" brawler, as he called
the general, in the White House in 1828, while he, a man of learning and experience, was continually reviled and ridiculed. Things
could only get worse, which they did, and he therefore concluded
that his public career was over.

One situation that developed early and further guaranteed disaster for his administration concerned the land and its occupation
by Indians. Of immediate concern was the problem of Georgia.
In 1802 that state ceded its western lands to the federal government on condition that Indian titles to them be extinguished.
But this agreement had not been implemented and Georgia
was becoming more and more insistent that something be done.
Historically the United States acquired Indian land through the
treaty-making clause of the Constitution, necessitating Senate ratification. Those treaties implied that the tribes were sovereign,

independent states, just like European powers. But the United States had no intention of recognizing the tribes as independent. Still, rather than seize the land and fight off resisting "savages," the government signed treaties that were rarely enforced and constantly violated by settlers who continued to move south and west and encroach upon Indian territory.

Adams had never been a friend of Indians or sympathetic to their pleas for justice. In 1802 he had sneered at what he called "moralists" who sided with them. Nor would he allow the British to set up an independent Indian buffer state in the Old Northwest during the negotiations in 1814 that drew up the Treaty of Ghent ending the War of 1812. And he defended Jackson when he crossed the border to attack Seminoles in Florida and sent them fleeing into the swamps.

John C. Calhoun, as secretary of war in the Monroe administration, proposed implementing a scheme first suggested by President Jefferson of moving the tribes west of the Mississippi River in a program of exchange. Under this plan about eighty thousand Indians would be relocated into the present states of Oklahoma, Kansas, Nebraska, and Iowa in return for the land they surrendered in the east. Indian rights to these new lands would be guaranteed, and those who declined to move could remain where they resided if they agreed to submit to state and federal law and control.

But Congress did not act on the scheme, so the Monroe administration addressed and satisfied Georgia's demands by concluding the Treaty of Indian Springs with the Creek Indians in 1825. The U.S. commissioners, Duncan G. Campbell and James Meriwether, who arranged the treaty, were in cahoots with Georgia officials but insisted that they had negotiated in good faith with "the Chiefs of the Creek Nation, in Council assembled." No one questioned their veracity and the Senate hardly discussed the treaty before approving it by a vote of thirty-eight to four, the day before Adams assumed the presidency. Actually, Chief William McIntosh, a leading headman and one-time speaker for the Lower Towns of the Creek Nation, along with seven lesser chiefs, agreed to sell all the land demanded by Georgia as well as two-thirds of Creek property in Alabama. But McIntosh and his cronies represented only eight of forty-six towns of the Nation and had no authority to conclude any such treaty. The entire transaction was fraudulent, and McIntosh was warned by headmen of other towns that he and his followers faced reprisals if they went ahead with the negotiations. One Indian chief actually stepped up to McIntosh and said, "My friend, you are about to sell your country; I now warn you of your danger." Indeed, on April 30, 1825, for his betrayal, a group of Creeks set McIntosh's house on fire and murdered him as he tried to escape the flames.

The Indian Springs Treaty stipulated that in return for land in the east the Creeks would receive an equal amount in the west, plus a bonus of $400,000 and annuities, most of which went to McIntosh and his friends. The Creeks were given eighteen months to vacate their land and no state survey of this territory would take place until September 1, 1826. In addition, McIntosh demanded protection from his Creek brothers, so the commissioners added an article that obligated the government to provide "protection against the incroachments, hostilities, and imposition, of the whites, and of all others." Unfortunately, as happened so often in the past, the government failed to keep its commitment and McIntosh paid with his life.

The Indian agent to the Creek Nation, Colonel John Crowell, immediately headed to Washington to inform the new president that the treaty had been fraudulently negotiated. He told Adams that the Indian commissioners, Campbell and Meriwether, "were both Georgians, and acted much more as such than as officers of the United States." Despite this alarming information, Adams went ahead and signed the treaty. After all it had been ratified by the Senate of the United States.

That was his first mistake.

On May 15, 1825, Adams learned of McIntosh's murder at an early meeting with McIntosh's son, Chilly McIntosh. Chilly handed the president a letter from the governor of Georgia, George Troup, that accused the government of responsibility for McIntosh's death and the likelihood of a general border war between whites and Creeks that Troup predicted would ensue. The governor accused the Indian agent John Crowell of having instigated the assassination and wanted him replaced. In defiance of the treaty and to hurry the process of procuring Creek land, Troup announced that he intended to open talks with the Indian chiefs for an immediate survey. He also vowed "revenge with a spirit," wrote Adams in his diary, "as ferocious as ever inspired by any Creek Indian." The president thought he must be a "madman." He then assured Chilly that he "was deeply depressed" by what had happened and advised him to consult the secretary of war, James Barbour.

By this time Adams had undergone a change of heart respecting the treaty he had signed. He realized that the Creek Nation in Georgia had been betrayed by scheming Indian chiefs and their white allies, led by Governor Troup. He also realized that he was working against the deadline of September 1, 1826, when a survey would begin, so he immediately directed Major Timothy P. Andrews, an officer stationed in Washington, to go to Georgia, investigate the charges against Crowell, and if proven true, to suspend the agent from office. At the same time Secretary Barbour ordered the rather "excitable" General Edmund Pendleton Gaines, commanding officer of the Eastern Department of the U.S. Army, to protect American citizens in the disputed area, restore the peace, and reunite the factious Creek tribe. Not surprisingly, when the excitable Gaines met the madman Troup, one outburst of threats and anger followed another in swift succession.

Adams and Barbour decided to dispatch a message to Troup explaining what had been reported to them and making it clear that "the President expects from what has passed . . . that the project of surveying their [Creek] territory, will be abandoned by Georgia, til it can be done consistently with the provisions of the treaty."

Troup shot right back: "If the president believes that we will postpone the survey of the country to gratify the agent and the hostile Indians, he deceives himself." The Georgia legislature also demonstrated what they thought of Adams's request by authorizing Troup to begin the survey immediately and establish Georgia law over the entire Indian country.

Meanwhile General Gaines summoned the Indians to meet with him at Broken Arrow. Seven hundred chiefs and headmen and over a thousand warriors attended the gathering. Gaines soon learned that

"49/50%" of the Creek people opposed the Treaty of Indian Springs. The leaders of the Nation had not signed the treaty, they said, no land had been sold, and no money would be accepted. Furthermore, the Creeks would not remove and would resist any attempt to use force to make them leave their land. All of this was reported back to Barbour along with a statement by Gaines declaring that he believed what the Indians had told him.

Gaines convinced Adams that the entire treaty negotiation had been one solid "mass of corruption and bribery." Forthwith Barbour notified Troup that "I am directed by the president to state distinctly to your excellency that, for the present, he will not permit such entry [into Creek land as threatened] or survey to be made." If they persist, Barbour made clear, General Gaines would be authorized to use military force to prevent it. Violators would be turned over to the judicial authority for punishment.

Troup backed off. But he savaged Gaines in the newspapers, accusing him of attempting to block the state's efforts to gain control of the land within its borders as promised by the agreement of 1802 and the Treaty of Indian Springs.

A delegation of Creek headmen then left for Washington in the hope of getting the administration to abrogate the fraudulent treaty. They were cordially met by the president.

"We should all meet in friendship," he said.

"We are glad to be here," responded Opothle Yoholo, a mixed blood, who spoke for his delegation. "Things have happened which have frightened us. We hope now that all will be well."

"That is my desire," agreed the president. "I have also heard of things which displease me. I expect you will be able to arrange things with the Secretary of War to the satisfaction of all."

The president then told them that it was most unlikely that Congress would abrogate the Indian Springs Treaty unless the Creeks signed a new agreement that would satisfy Georgia. After a long discussion the Indians prepared a new proposal in which they consented to give up their land east of the Chattahoochee but not any of their land west of that river. "We may as well be annihilated at once," they said, "as to cede any portion of the land West of the river."

According to this new proposal the United States promised to pay the Nation $200,000 when the Senate ratified the treaty, and $20,000 per year "in perpetuity or forever."

In proposing this concession the Indians apparently believed that they had assurances from both Gaines and Crowell that the river boundary would be acceptable. But the president subsequently opposed this river boundary. Since Georgia wanted everything within its borders, this agreement "would still leave the root of the controversy in the ground," he reminded Barbour. "It will be better to lay the treaty, as it is, before Congress, to decide upon it as they think proper, than to set it aside and form another, leaving the bone of contention still to be fought for."

Poor Adams. He was a novice both in Indian negotiations and in dealing with a truculent state and soon found himself out of his political depth in handling such matters.

He called a cabinet meeting and put the problem to the members. Clay said he had spoken with Daniel Webster, who warned against letting the question go to Congress because they would do nothing; and Clay himself agreed with the senator. Still, Adams pointed out, if Congress did nothing and the executive did nothing, the Treaty of Indian Springs would go into effect and the Indians would refuse to remove and bloodshed would surely result.

Barbour believed that the Indians had to be removed west, but as individuals, not tribes. He spoke of incorporating them within the states, placing them under the same law as whites, and ceasing the unenforceable practice of signing treaties with the various tribes. Since they were subject to state and national law there was no reason to resort to treaties.

But "don't you think," Adams asked, "that question would be made of the constitutional power of Congress to change so essentially the character of our relations with the Indian tribes?"

"I have no doubt there would," Barbour admitted, "but it will soon be unavoidably necessary to come to such a system."

Adams wrote that Clay thought the whole idea "impracticable; that it was impossible to civilize the Indians; that there never was a full-blooded Indian who took to civilization. It was not in their nature. He believed they were destined to extinction, and, although he would never use or countenance inhumanity towards them, he did not think them, as a race, worth preserving." They were inferior to the Anglo-Saxon race, Clay declared, and "their disappearance from the human family will be no great loss to the world."

Barbour was shocked by these opinions, "for which," wrote Adams in his diary, "I fear there is too much foundation."

The cabinet went on to suggest that a letter be written to the Georgia congressional delegation informing them of Creek refusal to surrender land west of the Chattahoochee and asking if that was agreeable. The letter was sent even though the cabinet members knew it would most likely get back "an insulting and violent refusal for an answer." It did.

Adams then sought the help of Thomas L. McKenney, head of the government's Indian Office, and Lewis Cass, governor of the Michigan Territory who had had a successful record in negotiating with Indians. He asked them to intercede and do what they could to end the stalemate and convince the Indians to surrender their Georgia land. Barbour also spoke to Senator Howell Cobb of Georgia, who was "in a state of high excitement and had threatened that unless we should concede this point [of obtaining all the land] Georgia would necessarily be driven to support General Jackson." Barbour then told the president that if Clay was correct and the Indians were headed for "inevitable destruction, what need was there for us to quarrel with our friends for their sakes, and why should we not yield to Georgia at once?"

"Because," Adams snapped in reply, "we could not do so without gross injustice. I consider Mr. Clay's observations of yesterday as expressing an opinion founded upon the operation of general causes, but not as an object to which we ought purposely to pursue. As to Georgia's being driven to support General Jackson, I feel little concern or care for that. I had no more confidence in one party there than in the other."

Adams, Barbour, McKenney, and particularly Cass badgered the Indian delegation to yield. Even the Cherokees advised them to give in. It got so bad that the "first chief of the deputation, Opothle Yoholo, attempted . . . to commit suicide." Hounded on all sides, the delegation finally capitulated and agreed to move the boundary line of the Chattahoochee to a more westerly branch of that river called Cedar Creek, a line "they had hitherto been unwilling to yield."

That done Adams authorized Barbour on January 24, 1826, to sign what became known as the Treaty of Washington with the Creek delegation. The treaty did not give Georgia all the land it demanded but as much as the Indians were willing to concede. Worse, it "guaranteed" to them such lands in Georgia that had not been ceded. In return the United States agreed to pay $217,600 plus a perpetual annuity of $20,000 and compensation for improvements on the land being surrendered. The Creeks were to vacate the territory by January 1, 1827.

In forwarding the treaty to the Senate, Adams said in his message that the Treaty of Indian Springs was unenforceable unless the country was prepared to go to war. In order to preserve the peace and in the interest of "justice and humanity," he recommended the ratification of this new treaty. In effect he recognized the sovereignty of the Creek Nation! He recognized that the Creek National Council had the same right as the U.S. Senate to accept or reject treaty negotiations carried on by their respective representatives. And he virtually told Georgia that this new treaty was the best they could hope to have and therefore to accept it gracefully and quietly.

But the Georgians did neither, and the Senate agreed with them. Negotiations were reopened and the Indians, after much harassment, were made to realize that they were holding out for a tiny parcel of land—and for what? Why not accept an additional $30,000 and cede the extra tract that would give Georgia most of what it demanded. After further badgering the Indian delegates reluctantly consented and the Senate ratified the modified treaty on April 22, 1826. Article 1 of the treaty declared the Treaty of Indian Springs to be "null and void."

Of the money subsequently paid out by the United States, $159,700 of it went to just twenty-four Creek chiefs and headmen and three Cherokees involved in the negotiations. Individual payments ran from $15,000 down to $200. Some of these chiefs were already very wealthy men and owned several plantations, taverns, ferries, three hundred or more slaves, and other property. Still their greed, like that of the whites, seemed insatiable. The remainder of the money went to the Creek Nation. Obviously "justice and humanity" had not been served.

But the politically perceptive secretary of state, Henry Clay, understood that the Creeks had scored an important victory: the government had provided official recognition that the Creek National Council could nullify a treaty. No Indian nation had ever before or would ever again compel the United States Senate to repudiate a ratified treaty.

As for all the other eastern tribes, Barbour gave up his idea of "incorporating" individual Indians into the states. Instead he suggested "forming them all into a great territorial Government west of the Mississippi." Adams thought the idea "full of benevolence and humanity." However, he doubted any such plan would work. "I fear there is no practicable plan by which they can be organized into one civilized, or half-civilized, Government."

Unfortunately the Treaty of Washington did not solve the problem. Georgia rejected it. One hundred and ninety-two thousand acres of land in Georgia remained in Creek possession, and Governor Troup wanted every last acre of it as promised by the agreement of 1802. Once September 1, 1826, arrived—the date under the Treaty of Indian Springs allowing surveys—Troup sent agents into the Indian country to stake out lands for sale. As far as he was concerned the Treaty of Indian Springs had not been superseded. He swore he would not receive "one square foot less than the entire country within the limits of Georgia." His legislature agreed and directed him to carry out the provisions of the Indian Springs Treaty. When Creek officials arrested some of the surveyors, Troup sent in the cavalry to recover them. "Georgia is sovereign on her own soil," he growled.

At a cabinet meeting Clay urged the necessity of using military force to protect the rights of the Indians. But Adams disagreed. "I have no doubt of the right," he said, "but much of the expediency, of doing so." The upshot was a decision to warn Troup against violating the law, assuring him that the president, who is charged with executing the laws, might be "compelled to employ, if necessary, all means under his control to maintain the faith of the nation by carrying the treaty into effect."

To which the governor speedily replied: "From the first decisive act of hostility, you will be considered and treated as a public enemy . . . and what is more, the unblushing allies of the savages whose cause you have adopted."

Adams seemed powerless before such defiance. So he decided to refer the entire matter to Congress—rather than commence a "conflict of arms"—and see what they could do to solve the problem. At the same time Barbour wrote to Troup "to warn the Georgians against proceeding."

In drafting his message to Congress, Adams first warned that a military clash between the national and state governments "would be a dissolution of the Union." But the cabinet took exception to this frightening threat and the president agreed to modify it. In his subsequent explanation of his position to Congress, he said that the Georgia authorities were acting in violation of the law, and although he had an obligation as chief executive to enforce the nation's laws, he would refrain from doing so in an effort to avoid civil war. Consequently he was submitting the problem "to the wisdom of Congress to determine whether any further act of legislation may be necessary or expedient to meet the emergency which these transactions may produce."

The House responded by recommending the purchase of the remaining Creek land in Georgia but agreed that the Treaty of Washington "ought to be maintained by all necessary and constitutional means." The Senate expressed only a perfunctory approval of the president's actions but clearly showed its sympathy for the state and its rights.

Ultimately the Creeks conceded that they had no recourse but to yield to Georgia's demands, and on November 13, 1827, they signed the Treaty of Fort Mitchel by which they gave up all their remaining territory within the state for an additional $27,491 plus $15,000 in goods and supplies.

At length, even the president came to agree with Georgia that Creek removal was necessary and just. His efforts to protect the Indians under the legal authority of the federal government gained him nothing but the hatred of all those southerners who lusted after Indian territory and could hardly wait for the next election to replace him in the White House with Andrew Jackson. Indeed, both slates of Georgia electors in the presidential contest of 1828 pledged themselves to the general with the full expectation that he would complete the policy of total removal of Indians from the entire southern region.

In the end no army was sent to protect Native Americans or their rights during the removal process. The Treaty of Washington pledged the government to provide federal protection but all Adams could provide were words that sounded encouraging but meant nothing. "We have talked of benevolence and humanity," he noted in his diary, "and preached them into civilization, but none of this benevolence is felt where the right of the Indian comes in collision with the interest of the white man. My own opinion is that the most benevolent course towards them would be to give them the rights and subject them to the duties of citizens, as a part of our own people. But even this the people of the States within which they are situated will not permit." He later admitted that Americans did more harm to the Indians than the British or the French or the Spanish combined. "These are crying sins for which we are answerable before a higher jurisdiction."

Adams meant well but he did not have the political dexterity, wisdom, or will to do what he knew was right.

8

Diplomatic Successes and Failures

The Creek debacle was not the only factor in the administration's ongoing loss of political strength and support. The building of a strong opposition was further enhanced by the president's steadfast refusal to rout out disloyal government employees and replace them with men who would help him implement his nationalistic program. Ability and integrity were the traits he required in making appointments, not political partisanship. Otherwise, he said, it would "make Government a perpetual and unremitting scramble for office. A more pernicious expedient could scarcely be devised."

The politically astute members of the cabinet, especially Henry Clay, did all they could to dissuade him from this self-destructive policy but they argued in vain. Under no circumstance would he denigrate the presidency by turning it into what he called an "electioneering machine." As a consequence each member of the cabinet had to go his own way with regard to appointments and Clay took pride in the fact that he managed a fair degree of control with the patronage under his supervision. "Nobody can say that *I* neglect my friends," he boasted. As a result his appointments were used by the Jacksonians to smear the entire administration with a charge of corruption. "The patronage of the government for the last three years," wrote Jackson in 1828, "has been wielded to corrupt every thing that comes within its influence, and was capable of being corrupted, and it would seem that virtue and truth, has fled from its embrace. The administrators of the Govt has stained our national character."

Adams also rejected any action that could be interpreted as electioneering. He told crowds that gathered to see and hear him to go home and attend their private duties. He refused to take part in the fiftieth anniversary of the Battle of Bunker Hill in Boston and was aghast when asked to appear at the opening of a Pennsylvania canal "so as to show myself among the German farmers and speak to them in their own language." He could speak German, and very fluently, but he would never use it to curry or seek favor. That violated his principles, he said.

Given Adams's character and personality it is not surprising that he later described his administration as a near total failure. The failure, if that is the word, was really brought on by his own inadequacies as a leader and politician. Even in foreign affairs, a field in which he held a normally sovereign command, he floundered.

The Panama Congress was the first disaster. Then, every effort he and his secretary of state attempted to advance Pan Americanism in Latin America was sidetracked or defeated by the growing Jacksonian forces, especially in the Senate where sympathetic understanding and agreement was vital. Nevertheless he and Clay did manage to block Colombian and Mexican efforts to seize Puerto Rico and Cuba from Spain, which, had it been successful, might well have ended in Cuban independence. Any takeover of these islands was seen as a direct threat to American security. "The United States," wrote Clay to Alexander Everett, the U.S. minister in Madrid, "are satisfied with the present condition of those Islands, in the hands of Spain, and with their Ports open to our commerce, as they are now open. This Government desires no political change of that condition." Mexico and Colombia begrudgingly backed off and the irony is that Adams and Clay, who had championed the liberation of Latin America, were responsible for delaying possible Cuban liberation.

Relations with Mexico were further damaged when the United States attempted to acquire Texas. Many Americans believed and argued that Texas was part of the Louisiana Purchase and that Adams had criminally relinquished it in the Adams-Onís Treaty of 1819 by which Florida was purchased but the western boundary of the Louisiana Purchase was fixed at the Sabine River instead of the Rio Grande. Several hundred American families had migrated to Texas under an agreement with Moses Austin and his son Stephen F. Austin in which they obtained sizable tracts of Texas land and a guarantee of home rule. In return they acknowledged Mexican authority in the area and promised to become Catholics.

Clay authorized Joel Poinsett, the first U.S. minister to Mexico, to offer one million dollars for Texas if the boundary was moved to the Rio Grande, and half a million if drawn at the Colorado River. The secretary also wished to throw in several warships but Adams vetoed that idea and instructed him "to offer only money." Unfortunately relations had soured between the two countries to such an extent that Poinsett never presented the proposal to the Mexican government. He himself was partially responsible. He committed several indiscretions by attempting to meddle in Mexican politics. As a consequence U.S.-Mexican relations went into a steep decline and never recovered during the next two decades.

Poinsett had one small success when he negotiated a trade agreement between the two countries. On July 10, 1826, he signed an agreement with Mexico on the basis of most favored nation, but ratification was held up until Adams and Clay had left office because of demands by Mexico that the United States reaffirm the Sabine River as the western border of the Louisiana Purchase.

Another boundary dispute that ended disastrously involved the northeast corner of the country between Maine and New Brunswick, Canada. Americans claimed the Aroostook area along the St. John River and one American settler on the Canadian side of the area was arrested for trespassing. The administration proposed arbitration in which the king of the Netherlands was invited to serve as arbitrator. But the king proved unacceptable to the governor of Maine, Enoch Lincoln, because he was viewed as Britain's ally. In a letter to Clay, Lincoln reminded him that the national government had no right to cede any part of a sovereign state without its consent. The temper of the letter, Adams noted in his diary, "is querelous [sic], testy, and suspicious." It only multiplied "the difficulties of the negotiations, and promises no good to the State." As a result "there is little prospect that it could now be settled upon reasonable terms." Lincoln, the president concluded, "is deeply infected with a disease which many of the Governors of the States are apt to catch—wanton assailing of the General Government, [and] overweening zeal for the interests of the State."

The dispute dragged on for several more years and finally resulted in a bloody clash—the Aroostook War—between American and Canadian settlers. Only then was the problem resolved with a compromise division of land in the Webster-Ashburton Treaty of 1842.

In conducting relations with foreign nations the Adams administration strove as its first object to obtain commercial advantages with other countries either under the broad rubric of reciprocity or, failing that, the most-favored-nation status. And a fair number of such treaties were signed, notably with Denmark in 1826, Mexico in 1826, the Hanseatic League in 1827, the Scandinavian countries in 1827, Prussia in 1828, and Austria in 1828. What Adams and Clay hoped to achieve was the establishment of free trade around the world.

One success that pleased Clay particularly resulted from a treaty signed in Washington on December 5, 1825, with Antonio José Cañaz, minister plenipotentiary of the Federation of Central America, in which the two nations agreed to import each other's products "on terms of entire equality." This, boasted Clay, "has been a model treaty." It provided for both reciprocity and most favored nation; that is, any benefit accorded other nations by one of the signatories would be granted automatically to the other signatory. It also bound both nations to the policy of "free ships give freedom to goods," a principle long advocated by the United States against the opposing policies of Great Britain and other European powers. Blockade and contraband were tightly restricted, and freedom of asylum, freedom of conscience, freedom of access to courts, and freedom to dispose of one's goods without interference were extended to the citizens of both nations. Unfortunately the Central American Federation began to break up almost immediately, and by the time Adams left office the federation no longer existed as a sovereign entity. It seemed as though even diplomatic successes ultimately ended in failure.

But the most spectacular diplomatic disaster of the Adams administration involved trade with the British West Indies. Because of the need for and value of sugar from these islands the trade had been most important to colonial Americans. But Great Britain ended it at the conclusion of the Revolution. By the 1820s that trade had declined in value to the American economy; still, it rankled that England imposed restrictions against foreign nations for its own benefit and those of its colonies. In retaliation the Congress in 1818 shut down American ports to those British vessels coming from ports closed to American ships. It was assumed, as Clay said at the time, that "when she is made to FEEL the injustice of her policy towards us, she will yield to more reasonable counsels."

Surprisingly, Britain yielded. Protests from her own colonists in the West Indies (Jamaica, Barbados, and several of the Leeward Islands) prompted the British government to revise its trade laws. In 1822, the restrictions were lifted. In response Congress reopened American ports. Adams, the secretary of state at the time, played a role in drafting the congressional legislation. But he overplayed his hand. He insisted that American ships be admitted to Britain's colonial ports on an equal basis with those of England and its colonies, a demand Great Britain summarily rejected. Relinquishing preference, said the Foreign Office, was tantamount to surrendering sovereignty.

Clay was sympathetic to the British position and tried to convince Adams that there was "more than plausibility in the British claims, and that we ought to concede something on this point." Besides, he himself enjoyed excellent terms with George Canning, the British foreign minister, and insisted that he could soon establish the "most perfect frankness & friendship" with "such an enlightened minister." Clay had seen a letter that Canning wrote to Christopher Hughes, U.S. minister to Sweden, that apparently pleased him very much. "I should fall in love with Mr. Canning," Clay wrote to a friend, "if I were to read many more of such letters from him." Adams noted in his diary that "Clay brought letters from C. Hughes and S. Smith of Baltimore. Hughes's enclosed copy of an answer received by him from G. Canning, which has put him out of his wits with exultation—his letter is a dissertation to prove that the whole science of diplomacy consists in giving dinners." For his part Adams did not trust Canning. He regarded him as "an implacable and rancorous enemy of the United States."

In consulting with various friends of the administration, such as Daniel Webster, Samuel Smith, John Holmes, and others, and inquiring of them whether the United States was asking too much "in insisting upon the introduction into the W. Indies of our produce on the same terms with that of Canada," Clay was counseled to withdraw the earlier demands by Adams. Before that could happen, however, William Hoskisson, the president of the British Board of Trade, proposed to Parliament a program of trade reform that would raise the British American colonies "as rivals to the United States . . . so as to render for the future their union with the mother country more cordial and efficient." In analyzing Hoskisson's address, Adams said that "the fear and jealousy of the United States . . . are unequivocally disclosed in many passages of the speech."

The administration decided to hold off responding until it received a clarification of exactly what the Hoskisson proposals entailed. And it came soon enough. When the new U.S. minister to Great Britain, Albert Gallatin, arrived in London, he received a curt note from Canning informing him that a British Order-in-Council of July 27, 1826, would exclude American ships from the West Indies, the Bahamas, Bermuda, and other British possessions in South America starting on December 1, 1826. Canada was exempted.

Adams called a cabinet meeting to consider the draft of instructions to Gallatin that he intended would be "a keen retort upon the sarcastic insolence of Canning's note." The president was convinced that in its application the Order-in-Council was directed "almost exclusively to the United States, and being only a covert mode of establishing regulations peculiarly adverse to them." There were "some nettles scattered through the note," and he wanted "to give him also some return for his gibes."

As finally written after prolonged discussion, the instructions directed Gallatin to inform the British that the United States was very anxious to "ascertain how their differences might be reconciled," believing that there must be "a misconception of each other's views." Gallatin was directed to assure the British that President Adams was perfectly willing to recommend to Congress the suspension of U.S. restrictions.

Dutifully Gallatin relayed this message to Hoskisson and Lord Dudley, then foreign minister, and received a typically haughty British response, as though they were speaking to inferiors attempting to curry favor. Hoskisson declared "that it was the intention of the British Government to consider the Intercourse with the British Colonies as being exclusively under its controul, and any relaxation from the Colonial system as an indulgence to be granted on such terms as might suit the policy of Great Britain at the time, when it might be granted."

That did it. Adams went to Congress and said that the British were unwilling to negotiate. There was no possible alternative, he went on, "but resistance or submission. . . . My own sentiment was in favor of resistance." The next step was up to Congress, but he himself advised that trade with British colonies be halted, both in the West Indies and North America. He presented all the documents involved in the dispute and asked for appropriate action.

Several proposals were put forward in both houses of Congress to implement Adams's request, all of which provided nonintercourse starting on September 30, 1827, unless the president received assurances that the West Indian ports would be reopened to American ships. But the Jacksonians, ever ready to embarrass the administration and demonstrate its incompetence, succeeded in passing a bill in the Senate that delayed any action that would close American ports or propound U.S. policy if Britain did not respond favorably. Their success in killing the Panama Congress encouraged them to adopt a similar tactic.

And it worked. The House refused to agree and so nothing was done. Under the circumstances Adams had no recourse but to reinvoke the restrictions of 1818 and declare American ports closed to trade with the British colonies. The president signed the order on March 17, 1827.

What a disaster. That John Quincy Adams could fail so miserably in these negotiations gave the Jacksonians more than enough ammunition to prove to the country that he was an overrated diplomat and a corrupt and incompetent president. "Our diplomatic President," the Jackson press sneered, had destroyed "colonial intercourse

with Great Britain" in an effort to advance the economic interests of
New England over the needs and interests of the rest of the country.

As for his even more corrupt secretary of state—that "black-
legged scoundrel from Kentucky"—he failed, reported the Calhoun
press with a straight face, because he uses English-made products
in preparing diplomatic instructions and when writing notes and
other correspondence. "O fie, Mr. Clay—*English* paper, *English* wax,
English pen-knives. Is this your *American* System? However let us
be just towards Mr. Clay in one respect—his playing Cards are of
American Manufacture. They are all made in New England—the
'land of steady habits.'"

Clearly these failures served to strengthen ties among the various factions supporting Jackson's election in 1828. Martin Van
Buren, the chief architect of the Democratic party, could hardly
restrain his delight. "*You may rest assured,*" he told a friend as the
West Indian negotiations collapsed, "*that the re-election of Mr. Adams
is out of the question.*"

9

The Tariff of Abominations

As the political condition continued to deteriorate for the administration, Clay felt obliged to go to Adams and complain that the postmaster general, John McLean, was actively aiding the Jackson coalition by "using perfidiously the influence and patronage of his office, which is very great, against the administration." But even though Adams judged McLean's conduct as "worse than equivocal" he would not remove him because no "specific fact" of malfeasance could be proved against him. Besides, McLean had "improved the condition of the Post Office Department since he has been at its head, and is perhaps the most efficient officer that has ever been in that place." But toward the close of his administration Adams finally had the evidence he demanded proving to him that "the conduct of Mr. McLean has been that of deep and treacherous duplicity. With solemn protestations of personal friendship for me, and of devotion to the cause of the Administration, he has been three years using the extensive patronage of his office in undermining it among the people. . . . McLean is a double-dealer."

Yet, despite this knowledge, Adams still did not remove him. He kept him on until the last day of his administration, and General Jackson, after his swearing-in as president, appointed McLean to the Supreme Court in appreciation for his considerable service to his election.

It is really impossible to think of any other president quite like John Quincy Adams. He seemed intent on destroying himself and his administration. By the same token it is difficult to think of a president with greater personal integrity.

Still, Clay kept after him to chop heads. He tried again with scandalous customhouse officers in Philadelphia and Charleston. Our party, the exasperated secretary bluntly informed the president, has "to contend not only against [its] own enemies, but against the Administration itself."

True, Adams responded. "They are no doubt hostile to the Administration, and the Collectors use all the influence of their offices against us by the appointment of subordinate officers of the same stamp against us." But I see "no reason sufficient to justify a departure from the principles with which I entered upon the Administration, of removing no public officer for merely preferring another candidate for the Presidency."

What idiocy! The administration was doomed, and nothing anyone could do would save it, all of which was demonstrated by the summer and fall state elections of 1827. The Democrats had built efficient political operations in the Northwest that brought excellent results for them in Ohio, Indiana, Illinois, and even Kentucky. What happened in Kentucky really shocked Clay. He admitted that it had "excited new hopes" among Jacksonians and "for the moment, created some depression amongst our friends." Even Daniel Webster was surprised. "I hope you have recovered from such a *shock*," he wrote to Clay. "There is, doubtless, much cause for regret."

When the Jacksonian-controlled Congress reconvened in December 1827, the wrecking of the Adams administration got under way with a vengeance. The first thing the House members did was replace the current proadministration Speaker with Andrew Stevenson of Virginia, an ardent Jacksonian. This was a vital move because the Speaker controlled committee assignments and could fill all the important committees with a majority of reliable and capable Democrats. The same procedure followed in the Senate, and Vice President John C. Calhoun was expected to break any tie vote that might result on key issues. "You will have seen the arrangement of our committees & the new Speaker," wrote one congressman. "A difference of opinion existed among the leaders but the course taken was conformable to the advice of Van Buren to them." As a consequence, the administration abandoned any claim to legislative leadership. "The opposition party," remarked one senator, "constitute in fact the *administration*. Upon it rests the responsibility of all legislative measures."

Adams took note of what was happening. "There is a decided majority of both Houses of Congress in opposition to the Administration—a state of things which has never before occurred under the Government of the United States." And it stung. Members of both houses, he wrote, were "bitter as wormwood in their opposition, indulging themselves in the warmth of debate in personal reflections as ungenerous as they were unjust," and yet they come to the White House "when invited, to the dinners; always ready to introduce their friends to the President, to partake of his hospitality, and to recommend candidates for every vacant appointment."

The antics of John Randolph in Congress were especially galling. He was allowed to stand up and spew forth "a farrago of commonplace political declamations, mingled with a jumble of historical allusions, scraps of Latin from the Dictionary of Quotations, and a continual stream of personal malignity to others, and of inflated egotism, mixed in proportions like those of the liquor which he now tipples as he speaks in the House, and which he calls toast-water— about one-third brandy and two-thirds water." But Randolph was very effective in his denunciations of the "corrupt bargainers," much to the delight of the opposition.

Besides regularly lambasting the administration on almost every issue to come before them the Jacksonians also set about finding the ways that would attract additional votes for their candidate in the 1828 election. Subsidizing and approving appropriations for lighthouses, harbor improvements, public buildings of one kind or another always engendered goodwill among their constituents. Land grants were another surefire route to state gratitude. Numerous bills were proposed throughout the session but only important or swing states received priority. Ohio, for example, which would cast sixteen electoral votes in the next election, received eight hundred thousand acres of land to assist its construction of canals, the sale of which was expected to yield about $1 million. Illinois and

Indiana were authorized to sell previously restricted land. And Alabama was awarded a four-hundred-thousand-acre land grant to improve navigation on the Tennessee, Coosa, Catawba, and Black Warrior Rivers. All the political techniques Adams steadfastly refused to condone or approve were authorized by the Democrats at a huge cost to the government.

The opposition then began what Adams regarded as a campaign of harassment. The Committees of Commerce and Ways and Means in the House, and the Finance Committee in the Senate, in seriatim, sent him identical calls for facts, opinions, documents, and other papers, thereby "requiring double labor to be answered. All these scrutinies are pursued, too, in a spirit of hostility to the Administration," Adams wrote, "and with purposes of factious opposition."

Naturally the Democrats argued their right to the information so that they could legislate intelligently and claimed that the president purposely dragged his feet in responding to their requests. When he did respond he was bad-tempered and querulous. True, Adams rarely let an opportunity go by to convey the rancor he felt over congressional treatment of his proposals and the discourtesies they regularly inflicted upon him.

But it was the tariff that demonstrated the lengths to which Democrats would go to horse-trade their way to the White House. The tariff, along with internal improvements and a strong national bank, were essential components of Clay's American System and the fundamental ideological basis of the Adams administration. Van Buren and his cohorts meant to strike a crushing blow at that system by turning the tariff issue into an electioneering gambit. The fiery radical southerner Thomas Cooper said it best when he wrote: "I fear this tariff thing, but by some strange mechanical contrivance or legerdemain, it will be changed into a machine for manufacturing Presidents, instead of broadcloths, and bed blankets."

The tariff problem developed when the Industrial Revolution took hold following the War of 1812 and a new era began that slowly converted the nation from a purely agricultural society to one that became increasingly industrial. A transportation revolution followed with the successful building of the Erie Canal in New York; the frontier receded westward, and an independent domestic economy blossomed. Although the Panic of 1819 slowed the process for several years, by the time of Adams's inauguration, industry and commence showed renewed vitality. Manufactures such as cotton and woolen mills multiplied throughout the decade. But increasingly these industries found stiff competition from abroad, particularly from Great Britain, and soon Congress was flooded with demands to revise the tariff rates and provide domestic companies the protection they needed to survive. At the same time producers of raw materials such as wool, hemp, and flax demanded protection.

Together these interests, representing thirteen states, sent more than one hundred delegates to a convention in Harrisburg, called by the Pennsylvania Society for the Promotion of Manufactures and the Mechanic Arts. On August 3, 1827, the delegates signed a memorial and petition to Congress demanding that the grievances of American farmers and manufacturers be redressed by increasing the schedule of tariff rates. Throughout the north the recommendations of the convention elicited strong support, particularly in such pivotal states as Pennsylvania and New York; but among southern states there was general opposition because higher tariffs invariably meant higher prices for the manufactured products they did not produce themselves.

Van Buren, as leader of the antiadministration forces, faced the difficult problem of placating southerners on the tariff question while at the same time soliciting support for Jackson from northerners. The result was the Tariff of 1828 or, as southerners dubbed it, the Tariff of Abominations.

The bill was concocted in the House Committee on Manufactures and it was the most lopsided and unequal piece of legislation imaginable. Virtually every item in it contained marks of political favoritism. It was especially friendly to farmers, less so to manufacturers since many of them were located in New England. A duty of ten cents per gallon was levied on molasses while that of distilled liquor was raised ten cents. Sail duck was set at nine cents per square yard, and hemp and flax were raised to forty-five dollars per ton to be increased five dollars annually until it reached sixty dollars.

But raw wool got the best deal of all. Seven cents per pound was levied plus a 40 percent ad valorem rate that would be raised five percent each year until it amounted to 50 percent. Manufactured wool—most of which was produced in New England—had nowhere near the protection it needed. A complicated schedule adjusted to the price range was proposed, which meant that manufacturers would have to buy their raw wool at ridiculously high prices and yet sell their finished product at a price that could not compete with what British manufacturers dumped on the market.

As reported out of committee it occurred to a number of partisans that the bill had been concocted to be defeated, the idea being that New England congressmen would be forced to kill the measure and the Jacksonians would claim that they tried to satisfy the needs of farmers and manufacturers but were prevented by the National Republicans. Southerners of course would be delighted and give the Jackson men full credit for understanding their problem and satisfying their demand.

Clay took one look at the schedule and declared that the Democrats "do not really desire the passage of their own measure." But, he reckoned, "it may happen in the sequel that what is desired by neither party commands the support of both."

Actually, the Democratic leadership always intended the bill to pass, despite all its abominations. As Silas Wright, Jr., Van Buren's representative and spokesman on the House committee that framed the bill, explained, the bill resulted from the necessity of accommodating the demands of "our friends." "Why did we frame the bill as we did?" he wrote. "Because we had put the duties upon all kinds of woolen cloths as high as *our own friends* in Pennsylvania, Kentucky & Ohio would vote them. Why did we put the duties upon Molasses so high? Because Pennsylvania and our friends west of that State required it to induce them to go for the woolens. The Hemp and flax duty was also inserted for the same reasons, and the duty on Irons are the Sine qua non with Pennsylvania." Thus the bill satisfied the needs of farmers and manufacturers in the middle Atlantic and western states, whose combined electoral vote could decide the election in Jackson's favor, and penalized those in New England for supporting Adams. As for the southern states, their expectations were disregarded since they had no intention of voting for Adams under any circumstance.

Many southerners, of course, believed that the bill was purposely abominable because their friends meant to defeat it. They therefore decided to help keep it intact, certain it would fail if unamended. "Its fate rests on our ability to preserve the bill in its present shape," declared Senator John Tyler of Virginia. "If we can do so, it will be rejected."

Foolishly, southern congressmen made their intentions known and it antagonized both westerners and New Englanders. "Can we go the *hemp*, iron, spirit and molasses," asked Daniel Webster, "for the sake of any woolen bill?"

Senator Thomas of Illinois went to the White House and told the president that the fate of the bill "was very uncertain. The professed object of the bill is the protection of domestic manufacturers, but there is compounded with it taxation peculiarly oppressive upon New England." As a representative of the West, Thomas explained to Adams that the Senate was nearly divided on the measure and that the outcome "will probably depend upon the votes of the members of Massachusetts." Since Webster's vote was reckoned as "doubtful," Thomas "came to intimate a wish to me," the president recorded, "that I would interpose to fix his indecision."

Interestingly enough Adams's next visitor was Webster himself who called to recommend the appointment of General William Henry Harrison as minister to Colombia, which the president subsequently approved. However, on this particular visit there was no discussion of the tariff—at least Adams did not record it. But two days later on May 8, five days before the final vote, Webster returned and they did discuss it, the senator at first admitting his indecision. Most probably the president urged him to vote approval, perhaps arguing that there were sufficient increases on the duties of hemp, raw wool, iron, flax, and molasses to satisfy large segments of the nation and provide basic assistance to important industries. Clay made the same pitch to his supporters. Pass the bill, Clay instructed his friends. "This is now my wish, and my advice."

The Jacksonian leaders also helped convince New England congressmen to vote for the bill. In the Senate they raised the woolens rate that made it more palatable to them. Such Democrats as Van Buren, Thomas Hart Benton, and John H. Eaton of Tennessee

supported the amendment and were joined by the two Massachusetts senators, Webster and Nathaniel Silsbee, and such other New
Englanders as Samuel A. Foote and Calvin Willey of Connecticut.
The House agreed to the change and on May 13 the entire package
passed. President Adams immediately signed it.

Northerners and westerners were delighted. Van Buren's newspaper in New York, the *Albany Argus*, congratulated the Congress
for giving "the country a national tariff, which protects with a just
and natural equality, all the great interests of the nation." The Kentucky *Watchtower* agreed, declaring that "the American people are
indebted" to their representatives for this notable piece of legislation.

Southerners, of course, raged. They believed their Jacksonian
friends had tricked them. Senator Littleton W. Tazewell of Virginia
supposedly collared Van Buren one day and angrily said: "Sir, you
have deceived me once; that was your fault; but if you deceive me
again the fault will be mine." A very disappointed and angry vice
president returned to his home in South Carolina and immediately
set about writing his *Exposition and Protest* in which he enunciated
his doctrine of nullification. A state, Calhoun contended, had a constitutional right to void any federal law within its borders that violated its basic rights. The South Carolina legislature published the
Exposition anonymously and the stage was set for a confrontation
that could threaten the very existence of the Union.

Passage of the Tariff of Abominations represented the final piece
of evidence that John Quincy Adams was headed for a massive
electoral defeat in the approaching election. The tone of the campaign had been set by the Democrats at the very beginning of his
administration when they charged it with corruption in defeating
the popular will in the House election of 1825. From that point the
character and conduct of the campaign went steadily downhill and
into the gutter. The most vile and unspeakable accusations were
hurled at both Adams and Jackson. Without question the election
of 1828 was the filthiest in American history.

10

"Skunks of Party Slander"

By the time Adams signed the "abominable" tariff the attacks on
him and his administration had grown so gross and vicious that he
reckoned his impending defeat as the greatest humiliation of his
life. His daily ritual reflected his mood. During the summer of 1828
he frequently devoted himself to "idle occupation." He would rise
about 4:15 A.M., write for an hour or two, then watch his "plants in
my pots and boxes" grow, visit the garden, read, and go "horseback
riding or swimming from a quarter to half an hour." Breakfast followed. The rest of the day was a normal routine of reading documents, seeing visitors, and transacting any business brought to him.
At night after dinner he would "visit my garden, and make trivial
observations upon the vegetation of trees till dark." After a "repose
in torpid inaction" for two hours he would retire.

The last winter of his residence in the White House varied the
schedule slightly. He gave up swimming and watching his plants
grow. Instead he sat for hours in the gloom and meditated on "the
severe trials of my life."

To add to his "trials" his son John Adams II asked permission to
marry his first cousin, Mary Hellen, who had recently broken her
engagement to John's elder brother, George Washington Adams,
because of George's strange and erratic behavior. The president
absolutely opposed the marriage but Louisa angrily insisted that
permission be given. Lacking the strength or will to quarrel with her

during this trying period Adams reluctantly gave his consent. John and Mary were married on February 25, 1828. What impact the marriage had on George Washington Adams can only be imagined in view of his subsequent suicide a year later. The couple produced a daughter the following December, the first child born in the White House.

Much of JQA's present misery came from the knowledge that the opposition had apparently convinced the American people that he and Clay had entered a "corrupt bargain" to "steal" the election from Jackson. Worse, the Democrats had erected "a party machine" dedicated to the "overthrow of aristocrats," in particular one John Quincy Adams. The approaching election must be viewed "by the sound planters, farmers & mechanics of the country," wrote one Jacksonian, "as a great contest between the *aristocracy* and democracy of America." Adams, Clay, and their cohorts represented the wealthy elite who would use the government to advance their selfish interests. Jackson, on the other hand, represented the "planters, farmers & mechanics"—in short the great masses of the American people.

In addition the Democrats created a vast network of newspapers across the nation that regularly hurled mud at virtually every member of Adams's administration. The *United States Telegraph*, a Washington journal of the Calhoun faction, was a good example. Samuel D. Ingham, "the pamphleteer and general-manager of the Jackson party in Pennsylvania," regularly contributed some of the most "delectable" gossip about Adams to appear in the *Telegraph*, gossip about his gambling, his swimming, his "kingly pomp," even his sexual activities. But Isaac Hill, the editor of the New Hampshire *Patriot*, outperformed all the other Democratic "peddlers of filth" by claiming that John Quincy Adams had pimped for the czar of Russia.

The details of this scurrilous story may have been supplied by Jonathan Russell, who had served with Adams on the peace commission in Ghent. It was published by Hill in a *Brief Sketch of the Life, Character and Services of Major General Andrew Jackson* and it contended that while minister to Russia, Adams "attempted to make use of a beautiful girl to seduce the passions of the Emperor Alexander and sway him to political purposes." The actual facts, as stated by Adams in his diary, were quite different. Martha Godfrey of Boston, he wrote, accompanied the family to Russia as chambermaid to Mrs. Adams and nurse to their son, Charles Francis. Shortly after their arrival Martha wrote a letter relating stories she had heard about "the Emperor's amours and gallantries." The letter was opened at the post office and "sent as a curiosity to the Emperor, who was diverted with it and showed it to the Empress." Then when the Empress's sister, the Princess Amelia of Baden, had expressed a desire to meet young Charles, he was sent one morning to her apartment in the palace accompanied by Martha. During the visit the emperor and empress happened to come by and spent about ten minutes talking with the child. "At the same time they had an opportunity of seeing the nurse, whose letter," Adams recorded, "had afforded them some amusement. It is from this trivial incident that this base imputation has been trumped up."

Trivial or not, the Jacksonian press delighted in tagging Adams as "The Pimp of the Coalition" whose extraordinary diplomatic successes in the past had at last been satisfactorily explained.

But the friends of the administration struck back by recounting the fact that Jackson had married Rachel Donelson Robards while she was still legally married to her first husband, Lewis Robards. Not until two years after their marriage did Robards finally obtain a divorce on the grounds of his wife's adultery and desertion. In all innocence Rachel and Andrew presumed that she had a divorce at the time of their marriage. They subsequently remarried. Still, the administration press labeled her a bigamist and Jackson her "paramour lover." When Rachel died of a heart attack on December 22, 1828, a little over a month after the election, Jackson blamed the published slander for her death, and he faulted Adams for not putting a stop to it.

Democrats countered by claiming that the president and his wife engaged in premarital sex. Duff Green, the editor of the *United States Telegraph*, led the assault on Louisa and was amazed when he was "denounced in the most bitter terms for assailing *female* character by those very men, who had rolled the slander on Mrs. Jackson under their tongues."

As the campaign sank deeper into political slime, even Jackson's mother was smeared. One newspaper contained the following notice: "General Jackson's mother was a COMMON PROSTITUTE, brought to this country by the British soldiers! She afterward married a MULATTO MAN, with whom she had several children, of which General JACKSON IS ONE!!!"

Other than sex, the charges against Adams covered a wide range of accusations, touching both his personal and professional careers. Representative Wright of Ohio came to him with a list of his "failures and offenses," starting with his supposed negative vote in the Senate on the Louisiana Purchase, his alleged willingness at Ghent to trade navigation of the Mississippi River for fishing rights off the eastern coastline, and his presumed suggestion that the president had the right to proceed with the Panama Mission without senatorial approval.

These charges, falsehoods, and misrepresentations, Adams complained, had been repeated over and over "in pamphlets, newspapers, handbills, stump-speeches, and dram-shop dialogues, throughout the Union, and, which, in the face of fifty refutations, the skunks of party slander"—and he named Samuel Ingham, John Randolph, John Floyd of Georgia, Alexander Smyth of Virginia, and others—"have been for the last fortnight squirting round the House of Representatives, thence to issue and perfume the atmosphere of the Union."

To prove the president's own individual corruption Democrats from various state organizations urged Congress to search diligently into his personal finances. "Push the enquiries about the money," demanded one New Englander. "Bring John Q's account before the Congress again if you can get them there—the whole from the commencement of the govt to the present day."

The Jacksonians obliged, and in calculating the pay John Quincy Adams received from the moment he left the United States to serve as minister to Russia in 1809 until he became secretary of state in 1817, they claimed it amounted to $105,000, or better than $12,000 a year. Proof, they argued, that the republic had rewarded him with an "exorbitant" sum of money for his services. Everything about Adams bespoke waste and extravagance. "We disapprove the kingly pomp and splendor that is displayed by the present incumbent," they protested.

To attract the German-speaking voters in Pennsylvania, handbills, pamphlets, and broadsides in German were published that charged the president with support for higher taxes. The Dutch in

New York, New Jersey, and Delaware were told that the friends of the administration called them "the Black Dutch, the Stupid Dutch, and the ignorant Dutch and other names equally decorous and civil." On the other hand, the Irish in Boston and New York were assured not only that Jackson was "the son of honest Irish parents" but that "Mr. Adams" and "the partisans of Messrs. Adams & Clay" had "denounced the Roman Catholics as bigots, worshipers of images, and declared that they did not read their bibles." Worse, "Johnny Q. the tory," was secretly conspiring to "UNITE CHURCH AND STATE after the manner of the English monarch." In the west, Jacksonians reversed their tactics and accused Adams of hobnobbing with Catholic priests and speaking Latin to them and their students. Or he was labeled a Unitarian, which in some parts of the United States was tantamount to calling a man an atheist.

Senator William Marks of Pennsylvania wanted to know what charities and pious institutions the president had contributed to, and Adams told him to mind his own business. The candidate was also asked about his "ideas of the Trinity," which he chose to answer. Quite frankly, he responded, he was neither a Trinitarian or a Unitarian. Moreover, he said he "believed the nature of Jesus Christ was superhuman; but whether he was God, or only the first of created beings, was not clearly revealed to me in the Scriptures."

Because of the Sabbatarian movement that had begun in the United States, which sought to ban all activities that desecrated Sunday, Isaac Hill singled Adams out as a violator by reporting that he was seen "travelling through Rhode Island and Massachusetts on the Sabbath, in a ridiculous outfit of a jockey." The president, Hill added, obviously had no sympathy for the religious sensibilities of Americans who believed that the Sabbath should be kept sacred and no one should travel or "gad about the countryside" on that day.

Perhaps the most damaging factor in the administration's approaching demise was the organizational superiority of the Democratic party. Hickory Clubs and Central Committees sprang up around the country and provided entertainment for the electorate at barbecues, rallies, and parades. They encouraged the crowd to wear hats with hickory leaves prominently displayed or carry hickory canes to show their party affiliation.

National Republicans sneered. "The multiplication of Jackson meetings, and the number of which they composed," commented Peter Force, editor of the administration's Washington newspaper, the *National Journal*, "are favorite themes with the Opposition papers. . . . If we go into one of these meetings, of whom do we find them composed? Do we see there the solid, substantial, moral and reflecting yeomanry of the country? No. . . . They comprise a large portion of the dissolute, the noisy, the discontented, and designing of society."

Adams himself took note of these raucous meetings. He was staying at Barnum's House in Baltimore when a pro-Jackson rally took place in the square adjoining his hotel. A member of the state legislature, the president recorded, "harangued the multitude for about three hours upon the unpardonable sins of the Administration and the transcendent virtues of Andrew Jackson." The orator was still speaking when Adams retired but the president could still hear his voice "like the beating of a mill-clapper." Unfortunately, he lamented, "ward meetings or committee meetings of both parties [occurred] everyday of the week. It is so in every part of the Union. A stranger would think that the people of the United States have no other occupation than electioneering."

Instead of sneering, the National Republicans would have been better advised to imitate their rivals and make a strong case for Adams as a caring, humane, and dedicated statesman of outstanding accomplishments. But the dour president was an impossible man to sell as a popular candidate. True, presidential candidates shunned campaigning in the first half of the nineteenth century, but even efforts to get him to mingle with the people and smile and wave at them failed repeatedly. On one occasion Adams journeyed to Philadelphia and a crowd cheered him when he landed at the wharf (although he did hear a few "Huzza for Jackson" from two or three voices) and followed him to the Madison House where he would stay for the night. They called to him to come out and talk to them. Finally he relented. "Fellow-citizens," he said, "I thank you for this kind and friendly reception, and wish you all good-night." With that he turned around and went back to his room, leaving them disappointed, if not annoyed or angered.

He had a better experience when he attended the commencement of the building of the Chesapeake and Ohio Canal. He and a
number of dignitaries proceeded to the place selected for breaking
ground. The president of the canal company gave a short speech
after which he handed a spade to Adams who plunged it into the
ground, only to hit the stump of a tree. After three or four futile
efforts to scoop up some soil the president pulled off his coat "and
resuming the spade, raised a shovelful of the earth, at which a general shout burst forth from the surrounding multitude."

And that was about as close as John Quincy Adams ever came to
pleasing a crowd who had come to see their president. Even on the
few occasions when he tried to be friendly, he faltered. For example,
on October 16, 1827, he attended a commemorative celebration in
Baltimore to mark the successful defense of the city against the
British during the War of 1812. He was of course asked to propose a
toast. "Ebony and Topaz," he called out. "General Ross's posthumous
coat of arms, and the republican militiamen who gave it."

If Adams was attempting to sound ridiculous he could not have
chosen a better toast. The spectators who heard him stared at one
another, searching for the meaning. When he saw their confusion
he immediately explained his meaning. But what he said only
intensified their astonishment. The expression came from Voltaire's
Le Blanc et Le Noir (a wickedly anti-Christian work the Democratic
press quickly pointed out), in which Ebony represented the spirit
of evil, exemplified by the British Commanding General Robert
Ross whose coat of arms received a posthumous addition by King
George III, while Topaz represented the good spirit symbolized by
the militiamen.

Democrats roared with laughter. Initially, said the *New York
Evening Post*, "we supposed it to have been the production of some
wicked Jacksonian wag who had undertaken to burlesque the
clumsy wit and unwieldy eloquence of the ex-professor." But no, it
came from "Old Ebony" himself. Duff Green admitted he was not
as deeply read in "Oriental literature" as the president and therefore
would reserve comment.

National Republicans were appalled. "I wish Mr. Adams's ebony
and topaz were submerged in the deepest profound of the bathos,"

Charles Hammond, editor of the Cincinnati *Gazette* told Henry Clay. "You great men have no privilege to commit [such] blunders."

Recognizing the essential need for better organization, a number of leading National Republicans tried to fashion a party that could appeal to intelligent voters. They knew they had a superb program, one that would benefit the electorate in all sections and classes of the country. And they knew they had a candidate of proven talent, integrity, and experience. To put it all together Henry Clay and Daniel Webster urged their friends to forget the "old political landmarks" and join together in support of a modern party that would be responsive to the fast-changing economic needs of the American people.

But party organization requires money. "It seems to me," Clay wrote to Webster, "that our friends who have the ability should contribute a fund for the purpose of aiding the cause." So, while Webster pursued what money was available, Clay directed its distribution. With these contributions a number of newspapers were begun and older ones subsidized. In Washington the *National Intelligencer* and the *National Journal* were strong administration sheets. Elsewhere the New York *American, Niles' Weekly Register*, a Baltimore organ, the New Jersey *Patriot*, the Cincinnati *Gazette*, the Kentucky *Reporter*, the Illinois *Gazette*, and the Missouri *Republican* attempted to counter the stinging propaganda spewed forth daily by the Jackson press. These journals naturally capitalized on Jackson's reputation as a brawler, duelist, and home wrecker. They spread the gory details of the general's marriage, his duel with Charles Dickinson over a horse-race wager in which he killed Dickinson, and his barroom brawl with Thomas Hart Benton and his brother, Jesse, back in 1813.

Among the most potent publications issued by the National Republican press was the "Coffin Handbill," a broadside conceived by John Binns, editor of the Philadelphia *Democratic Press*, that depicted six large black coffins over which were inscribed the names of six militiamen whom General Jackson put to death during the Creek War. Actually, these men had deserted Jackson's army, stolen supplies from the commissary, and hatched a mutiny among two hundred militiamen. They were tried by a court-martial and ordered to be shot. When the handbill appeared the Jackson Central

Committee in Tennessee immediately accused Adams and Clay of conceiving this despicable publication in a vain attempt "to strip the honored laurel from [Jackson's brow.]"

Jackson's mistreatment of the Indians, his execution of two British subjects in Florida during the First Seminole War, and his disastrous tenure as territorial governor of Florida after its acquisition from Spain were all duly circulated throughout the country. The National Republicans took great pains to prove that the general's ordinances as governor were so dreadful that Congress was obliged to abrogate every one of them. Jackson was also accused of participating in the conspiracy of Aaron Burr in which it was alleged that Burr had tried to dismember the Union in order to create an empire for himself in the Southwest.

The journals of the National Republican party also urged the several states to hold conventions—just like the Democrats who nominated Jackson with Calhoun as his running mate—and place Adams's name in formal nomination. "What party is so poor as not to have a *convention* in these times," declared William C. Rives of Virginia. Even in the South, where Adams's chances were next to hopeless, administration partisans held conventions in Virginia, North Carolina, and Louisiana and placed John Q. Adams at the top of their ticket along with Richard Rush as his vice president.

One political development that did occur toward the close of the administration that some thought boded well for Adams was the sudden and explosive outbreak of Anti-Masonry in western New York. It seems that a mason by the name of William Morgan had become disaffected with the fraternity and decided to write a book and reveal Masonic secrets. When he resisted all persuasion to desist, he was hustled into a carriage, then driven to Fort Niagara, where he was held for several days before being drowned in the Niagara River.

Within weeks Morgan's disappearance created a wild outburst of resentment in New York against all masons. His supposed murder was seen as a conspiracy of elite aristocrats, bound together by secret oaths and handshakes and committed to criminal acts to gain wealth and power. They were accused of taking the law into their own hands, of respecting no law except whatever satisfied their interests. Meetings were held to voice public anger and resentment, and the furor promptly spread to states in New England and the West. Before long, an Anti-Mason party was formed with the purpose of ousting masons from all three branches of government.

At the height of this excitement it was discovered that Andrew Jackson was a "grand king" of the Masonic Order and it severely damaged his reputation throughout the "infected area." The Democrats tried to counter the blow by accusing Adams of being a mason, but the president categorically denied it. "I state that I am not, never was, and never shall be a freemason," he declared. Unfortunately it turned out that Henry Clay was a mason, which the Jacksonians immediately exploited. Clay's friends begged him to resign from the organization so that the president's political gain on the issue would not be lost, but he steadfastly refused.

Another development that had political ramifications took place in Philadelphia in July 1828. This was the formation of a Workingmen's Party comprised of laborers, merchants, physicians, businessmen, lawyers, politicians, and others, and they demanded legislative action against those who monopolized "the wealth creating powers of modern mechanism." Both the Democratic and National Republican parties recognized the danger this new party posed so they both ran candidates as Workingmen. Interestingly, when the final returns were tabulated in 1828, the Democrats won the city and county, including all the Workingmen candidates who also ran on their ticket. One man had a simple explanation for this result. The Democrats, he said, enjoyed "superior management and activity," giving them "the machinery" by which to succeed.

Superior management! And with it the people were about to destroy the administration of a man who had, he said, devoted his "life, and all the faculties of my soul to the Union, and the improvement, physical, moral, and intellectual, of my country." Still, he understood that "in the excitement of contested elections and party spirit . . . men of intelligence, talents, and even of integrity upon other occasions, surrender themselves to their passion."

The election of 1828 ended with politicians urging a massive turnout by the electorate in an effort to pile up large majorities for their candidates. "TO THE POLLS!" commanded Duff Green in his *United States Telegraph*. "To the Polls! The faithful sentinel must not sleep—Let no one stay home—Let every man go to the Polls—Let not a vote be lost—Let each Freeman do his duty; and all will triumph in the success of JACKSON, CALHOUN and LIBERTY."

Voting procedures varied in the twenty-four states. In the past four years many states had changed their constitutions to provide universal white manhood suffrage. But two states, South Carolina and Delaware, retained the practice of allowing their legislatures to choose the electors.

Voting began in September and ended in November. When all the ballots had been counted they showed that John Quincy Adams, as many predicted, had been decisively defeated. Jackson won 178 electoral votes, which came from every state south of the Potomac River and west of New Jersey. Adams carried New England, Delaware, New Jersey, and most of Maryland. New York divided its vote and gave 20 electoral votes to Jackson and 16 to Adams.

Some 1,155,340 white males voted in a total population of 13,000,000. Of that number Old Hickory polled 647,276 (approximately 56 percent of the total vote cast) to Old Ebony's 508,064. Democrats, of course, were jubilant over their victory and insisted that it was the outpouring of ordinary citizens who affirmed their belief in popular democracy by voting for one of their own. It was a victory, they said, of democracy over aristocracy.

The National Republicans rightfully credited their defeat in large part to the absence of a fully organized party. "Organization is the secret of victory," announced the *New York American.* "By the want of it we have been overthrown." But that was not the only reason. Although Adams had everything an intelligent voter could want in a candidate, he was by all accounts a political disaster in this new age of democratic excitement, an age with hundreds of thousands of newly enfranchised voters. He had little personal appeal; he abhorred public demonstrations on his behalf; and he was seen as a sectional candidate who espoused the programs and goals of the wealthy. More than anything else, he supposedly struck a "corrupt bargain" with Henry Clay in 1825. That single issue went a long way in bringing about his defeat.

Adams himself was devastated by the loss. The "skunks of party slander" had made his "character and reputation a wreck." Still, "in looking back," he confided to his diary, "I see nothing that I could have avoided, nothing that I ought to repent. I have nothing further to hope from man," he sighed. "My only trust is in the Divine Disposer; and of Him all that I can presume to ask is to stay the hand of His wrath, to grant me fortitude to endure, and, in disposing of me as to Him shall seem wise and good."

The new year, 1829, opened for Adams "in gloom." The dawn was overcast. As he sat at his desk writing, his shaded lamp went out for want of oil but, he said, it marked "the present temper of my mind."

He spent the next two months closing down his administration. He took particular note of the day the Congress counted the electoral ballots and declared Andrew Jackson the seventh president of the United States. It was the same day the president-elect arrived in the city, dressed in black and wearing a weeper around his hat to honor the recent death of his wife, Rachel. As the weeks passed Adams also noted that Jackson had "not thought it proper to hold any personal communication with me since his arrival." So Adams sent the city marshal to the general to inform him that "I should remove with my family from the house, so that he may, if he thinks proper, receive his visits of congratulation here on the 4th of March."

It rankled that Jackson did not pay him the courtesy his office deserved. "His avoidance has been noticed in the newspapers," Adams recorded. Duff Green said the reason "of this incivility" was the fact that Jackson knew, wrote Adams, that "I have been personally concerned in the publications against his wife. . . . This is not true. I have not been privy to any publication in any newspaper against either himself or his wife." Whatever reason the general may have had, Adams felt that this "incivility" obliged him to depart from the tradition of the outgoing president attending the inauguration of his successor. He discussed the matter with his cabinet and all but Rush agreed with him. So on March 3 at 9 P.M. he left the White House with his son and joined his wife, who had already moved to their temporary home at Meridian Hill, which was two miles from the Capitol. He and his father were the only two departing presidents who, deeply hurt and disillusioned, deliberately boycotted the inauguration of their successors.

"I can yet scarcely realize my situation," he wrote on the day Jackson was sworn into office. Then he prayed for direction from the "Divine Disposer." "From indolence and despondency and indiscretion may I specially be preserved!"

He did not know it, of course, but another important and perhaps even greater phase of his career still lay ahead.

11

Congressman John Quincy Adams

Louisa Johnson Adams hated her life in the White House. It was almost as bad as when she lived in St. Petersburg. The house was cold and drafty, the furniture worn and uncomfortable. Over the years she had grown resentful of her husband's ambition and she never quite recovered from the trauma she suffered in leaving her two elder sons at home while she accompanied her husband to Russia with Charles Francis. Guilt continued to torment her as she watched the steady mental decline of George and John II. As a result she suffered periodic nervous spells that prostrated her for days. Living with John Quincy Adams all these years had taken its toll; still, like most women of her age, she remained faithful and tried to accommodate his every wish and need. Deep down she loved him, and he her. Unfortunately he rarely showed it, especially those moments when she needed him the most.

Her agony can well be imagined when she learned of the death of her eldest son, George Washington Adams. The young man had been summoned to Washington to help in the removal of the family to Quincy. His dissolute ways, his indifference to his work, and his disposition to gamble prompted a stern pronouncement from the father that once home George would live in close association with the family where his behavior could be monitored.

And that probably finished the young man. He had recently impregnated Eliza Dolph, a young chambermaid of the Welch family where he was living, and the thought of what his father would say, plus the thought of having him constantly hammering away at him to live a disciplined and moral life, was more than he could endure. Several times in his despair he hinted at suicide. On April 30, 1829, he took a steamboat to New York and vanished—presumably overboard. A hat and a cloak lay on the deck. A month later his remains washed ashore off Long Island Sound.

George's death paralyzed both parents. John Quincy was prostrate with grief. He had lost both the presidency and his eldest son in a matter of months. "Blessed God," he implored. "Forgive the wanderings of my own mind under its excruciating torture." Then, John Quincy cried out, "My God, my God, why hast thou forsaken me." As far as he was concerned his life was over. His "broken and contrite spirit" now confessed that all his hopes on earth had been destroyed. I have been "deserted by all mankind," he wept. "I have nothing left to rely on but the mercy of God."

It took weeks before the sixty-two-year-old man could begin to function. He struggled back to Quincy. The self-pity, the blame he assigned to himself for all these tragedies, and his naturally pessimistic temperament aged him considerably. But there was one bright moment. It occurred on September 3 when his youngest and most talented son, Charles Francis, married Abigail Brown Brooks, the daughter of one of New England's wealthiest men. Charles would prove to be the kind of son John Quincy always hoped for and feared he would never have. Although, if truth be told, even Charles did not completely measure up to what was expected of him.

Not that this happy marriage could dispel Adams's newest worry about John II. Alcohol, the family's demon, had claimed another victim and would eventually destroy John's life. The father could scold and warn but it hardly helped.

Feeling used up and infirm, John Quincy was genuinely surprised when a number of Quincy neighbors and the editor of the Boston newspaper, *Courier*, suggested that he consider running for Congress. When it was seriously proposed to him he quickly assured his callers that he would not seek office and had "not the slightest desire to be elected." Still if the people should demand it of him, well, then, he might "deem it my duty to serve."

That was enough to set the campaign in motion. The current congressman, Joseph Richardson, chose to retire, which made the election of the ex-president all the easier. And to his utter amazement and delight, John Quincy Adams won by a two to one margin over two opponents. He received 1,817 votes against 373 votes for the Democratic candidate and 279 for the candidate of the still active Federalist party in Massachusetts. "My election as president of the United States," he admitted, "was not half so gratifying to my inmost soul." Although the election took place in November 1830, he would not take office until a year later when the Twenty-second Congress convened on December 5, 1831.

All of a sudden life took on new meaning. "I am launched again upon the faithless wave of politics," he wrote. His interest in botany and literature were rekindled, he began writing poetry once more, and he even consented to give a Fourth of July oration. "My election to Congress was a *call*," he wrote, "unsolicited, unexpected, spontaneous." As such, to a man like John Quincy Adams it was a heaven-sent gift, a command to return to duty.

Years later he was asked his rules for surviving the disappointments and tragedies of life. He replied that there were three: regularity, regularity, regularity. The regular activity of body and mind guided by self-discipline and Christian prayer, he declared, helped him overcome depressions and frustrations, the unavoidable and inevitable components of life.

As always, he turned to his responsibilities as a congressman with great zest and determination. And, after arriving in Washington, his colleagues treated him with great respect, which helped him overcome his apprehensions. He had hoped to be placed on the Committee on Foreign Affairs, where his knowledge of the history and languages of the European world could be used to advantage. But the crafty Jacksonians assigned him to the chairmanship of the Committee on Manufactures in which he would have to grapple with an issue that now threatened to provoke a confrontation between the national government and South Carolina over the tariff.

For several weeks, and in conjunction with Jackson's secretary of the treasury, Louis McLane, Adams and his committee prepared a new bill that they hoped would be more amenable to the south. The resulting Tariff of 1832—or "Adams tariff"—lessened some of the "abominations" of the 1828 bill by deleting a few articles from the schedule and lowering duties on noncompetitive goods. But it retained a high rate of protection on everything else and President Jackson signed it.

It was not good enough. The legislature of South Carolina called a convention that subsequently declared the tariffs of 1828 and 1832 violations of its sovereign rights as a state. The convention nullified the tariffs and forbade the collection of customs duties within its borders. If the national government imposed compliance with the tariff law by military force, the convention proposed that the state secede from the Union.

The real and frightening danger to the Union caused some men to think that perhaps John Quincy Adams might be the one person to prevent civil war. "It was ridiculous to hear men who but three years ago were abusing Mr. Adams, with all their might," wrote Congressman Edward Everett, who are now suddenly aware "that he is the only man who can save the Union."

The new Massachusetts congressman was also placed on a committee to investigate the Second National Bank, whose practices Jackson had questioned. Adams thought very well of the bank, and when its president, Nicholas Biddle, requested a renewal of its charter four years before the present charter was due to expire, Adams spoke in its favor. To his amazement and shock, President Jackson vetoed the bill and ran for reelection in 1832 on a ticket calling for the bank's destruction. Henry Clay who championed the bank ran against the president but was overwhelmingly defeated. The Anti-Masonic party also entered the contest. At first it considered nominating Adams at its national nominating convention, the first such convention in American history, but finally opted for William Wirt.

Jackson's victory doomed the national bank; then he removed the government's deposits and placed them in various state banks. Under the direction of the defeated Henry Clay the Senate passed a resolution of censure against the president. In his "Protest" message of response Jackson advanced the concept that the president is the only elected officer of the national government who represents all the people and is responsible to them. It was a novel concept that set forth the primacy of the chief executive among the three branches of government.

Adams would not support the censure, much as he loathed Jackson, because it was the kind of harassment he himself had experienced as chief executive. Besides, he felt that such action only demeaned the office.

During the debates over the removal of the deposits and the censure of the president various groups around the country—National Republicans, Federalists, friends of the bank and internal improvements, states' righters, some nullifiers, and all those who abominated Jackson's high-handed methods and claim of primacy—allied themselves and adopted a new name for their coalition. Thereafter they were known as Whigs, supposedly in imitation of their revolutionary forebears who contended against the crown. Adams disliked the name because in England it was the party of aristocrats. Besides, it made no sense to adopt a British name in America, he said. Still, he remained loyal to the new party whatever its name.

More important was Jackson's handling of the nullification controversy. On December 10, 1832, he issued a proclamation to the people of South Carolina warning them against carrying out the threat of secession. "Disunion by armed force is *treason*," he lectured. "Are you really ready to incur its guilt?" As far as he was concerned, "the power to amend a law of the United States, assumed by one State, is *incompatible with the existence of the Union*."

Adams agreed. He said the message "contained much sound constitutional doctrine, more indeed than properly belonged to the source whence it originated." But when Clay and Calhoun worked out a compromise tariff to end the controversy, a tariff that would lower the protective rates over a ten-year period, Adams was outraged. As chairman of the Committee on Manufactures he wrote a long report, protesting the failure of the compromise measure to adequately protect manufacturers. Nevertheless, the president signed the bill and the nullification controversy ended peaceably.

Adams also disagreed with the president over the question of internal improvements. Jackson had vetoed the Maysville bill, which would have extended the national road through Kentucky. To JQA "the constitution is but one great organized engine of improvement—Physical, moral, political."

Adams's bitterness toward Jackson resurfaced when his beloved Harvard decided to bestow an honorary degree on the president and Adams was asked to attend the ceremony. He categorically refused. "I could not be present to see my Darling Harvard disgrace herself by conferring a Doctor's degree upon a barbarian and savage who could scarcely spell his own name."

At this time Adams was also asked to run as the Anti-Masonic candidate for governor of Massachusetts and he consented. It turned out to be a three-way contest that required a majority vote for election. Adams came in behind John Davis, the Whig candidate, and rather than submit to a face-off he withdrew in Davis's favor.

Another shock came when his second son, John Adams II, died of alcoholism on October 23, 1834. The father had rushed to his son's bedside when he learned of his illness but young John had already sunk into a coma. He was only thirty-one. Two years earlier, John Quincy's younger brother, Thomas Boylston Adams, also died of alcoholism, leaving behind a widow and large family. This curse had certainly locked the Adams family in its fearful grip. JQA's two sons and two brothers had succumbed to it. Now only Charles remained. Fortunately, the young man, like his father, escaped the disease. "All my hopes of futurity in this world are now centered on him," wept the old man.

Once again Adams cried out about the terrible personal and political woes he had suffered in the past few months and he pleaded with Providence to give him the strength to continue to function and remain active. So many men had tried to bring him down, he complained. And he named them: Jackson, Crawford, Calhoun, Webster, Jonathan Russell, Timothy Pickering, and countless others. They have "used up their faculties in base and dirty tricks," he recorded in his diary, "to thwart my progress in life and destroy my character." What had he done in response? "I have returned good for evil. I have never wronged any one of them." And that was his great mistake. I should have struck back, he said—hard.

Adams buried his sorrow in his diary and in concentrated congressional work. Surprisingly he sided with Jackson over a dispute that involved a fortification bill to which Daniel Webster had taken exception. In a Senate speech Webster opposed the bill because it placed a great deal of unrestricted money in the president's hands. Besides, there was no real danger of war, he declared. Even had an enemy landed on U.S. soil and was battering down the walls of the Capitol, he continued, he would vote against it. The preservation of the Constitution meant more to him than forty Capitols.

It was a very foolish speech, and John Quincy Adams immediately pounced on the author. JQA had little regard for the so-called God-like Daniel, and in a three-hour House harangue he leveled one "deadly thrust" after another at him. Webster had been instrumental in preventing Adams's possible election to the Senate by the Massachusetts legislature and in a way this public pillorying evened the score. Several times in the course of the speech Adams made reference to actions in the upper chamber and was repeatedly called to order by the chair. But the Democrats delighted in seeing Webster verbally pummeled and they cheered Adams on.

The climax of the speech was memorable. There was only one thing left for those who refused an appropriation if the enemy was at the gates of the Capitol, said Adams. *"I say, there was only one step more, and that a natural and an easy one—to join the enemy in battering down these walls."*

The House exploded with wild shouts, whistles, applause—and hisses. The Whigs could hardly believe what Adams had done. The Democrats, of course, congratulated him and said it was a notable speech from one not generally credited for spell-binding oratory. Thereafter John Quincy Adams was known in the Capitol as "Old Man Eloquent."

He himself took great pride in his feat. I "demolished the speech of Webster, drove him from the field, and whipped him," he gloated.

Adams also disappointed his party by supporting Jackson's foreign policy with respect to the president's demand for payment owed to Americans by the French as a result of the spoliations of U.S. commerce during the Napoleonic Wars. Jackson resorted to threats but he did convince the French to pay what they owed. With respect to other issues, however, Adams was decidedly hostile. He opposed the administration's positions on internal improvements, protective tariffs, the national bank, and removal of the Indians. Still his party could never count on his vote. He further disappointed Whig colleagues by maintaining his ties with the Anti-Masonic party until it declined and finally disappeared as new issues and a new national agenda emerged in the late 1830s and 1840s.

The most important new issue involved slavery and its expansion. During the Jacksonian era any number of organizations arose to advance women's rights, temperance, world peace, the strict observance of the Sabbath, and reforms of penal and mental institutions, among others. But unquestionably the most important of these movements was the driving impulse to abolish slavery.

Antislavery was not novel. For decades various religious groups, particularly Quakers, had advocated abolition. But fired by the enthusiasm and dedication of those caught up in the religious frenzy of the Second Great Awakening that swept the country during the first half of the nineteenth century, and outraged over the slaughter of slaves in the Denmark Vesey Conspiracy in 1822 and the Nat Turner Rebellion in 1831, the movement became militant and produced a small army of abolitionists who were determined to wipe out this "peculiar institution." The most radical of these reformers called for its immediate extinction. Others, less fanatical, wished simply to halt its expansion westward into the territories. One thing seemed certain, however: the slavery question had the potential to ignite civil war.

Petitions began to flood the Congress to terminate slavery in the District of Columbia and the territories, most of which were simply tabled and forgotten. But that only incited radical abolitionists into increasing their demands and threats. As a consequence southern congressmen demanded that all discussion of slavery in whatever form be terminated in Congress. To their minds, a "gag" resolution would quell the demand for any action by the federal government.

John Quincy Adams had shown little concern about slavery during his early career, and although he had no love of the institution he in no way condemned it. Like many others, he acknowledged that compromises had been necessary to produce the Constitution and one of the most important was the recognition of slavery and the right of slave-holding states to count three-fifths of their slaves as part of their population for purposes of representation in the House of Representatives. Still, to Adams the obligation to respect and obey the law of the land did not mean he had to assist slavery's expansion or gag congressmen who wished to express their opposition to it, or, most importantly, abolish a citizen's right of petition. As the issue continued to inflame the country Adams came to realize that the question of slavery threatened the very existence of the Union. And that he could never abide. "The real question convulsing the Union," he wrote in a statement that was later echoed in Lincoln's "House Divided" speech, "was whether a population spread over an immense territory, consisting of one great division of all freemen, and another of masters and slaves, could exist permanently together as members of one community or not."

In addition he began to see slavery as the root cause of all sectional divisions, be it the tariff, internal improvements, Indian removal, public land, territorial expansion, whatever. And he claimed that the Democratic party was responsible for protecting slavery and preventing its free discussion in Congress. True, in creating that party, Van Buren had called for a union of southern planters and northern republicans by which northerners were presumably required to support their slave-owning southern colleagues as the price for national victory at the polls. But to Adams that union meant that the Democratic party had in fact become the party of slavery. This distorted view was later accepted and advanced by many historians who were disillusioned by the bank war, the removal of the Indians, and the attempts to stifle free speech. Actually, any number of Democrats, north and south, opposed slavery and its expansion. Indeed, in the election of 1848 the Free Soil party ran the Democrat Martin Van Buren for president—and his running mate was JQA's son, Charles Francis Adams.

In a very real sense Adams's hatred of the South and Democrats in general stemmed from his desire to punish them for having wrecked his administration. "The slave-monger brood," he wrote, were "linked together with the mongrel Democracy of the North and West." Jackson, "the deepest, the cunningest, and the foulest rascal of them all," along with Calhoun, Crawford, and countless other Democrats, had maligned his character and conspired against him, making it impossible for him to govern and enact his program of economic, intellectual, and cultural betterment for the nation. Now he could get even. By attacking slavery he could inflict the revenge he so desperately sought for the role played by Democrats, north and south, in ruining his presidency.

Still that motive alone does not entirely explain his present attitude toward slavery. Although it had taken many years it is possible that, following the massacres of blacks during the Denmark Vesey Conspiracy and the Nat Turner Rebellion, along with the race riots of the 1830s, he finally came to the realization that something had to be done about the "peculiar institution." Not that he joined the abolitionists or agreed with their tactics. He opposed the idea of emancipating slaves in the District of Columbia because he did not believe Congress had the constitutional authority. And he showed only contempt for radical abolitionists who would actually destroy the Union to achieve their goal. For example, William Lloyd Garrison, the brilliant abolitionist editor, later called the Constitution "a covenant with death and an agreement with hell." He even burned the Constitution at a public rally. "So perish all compromises with tyranny," he thundered.

That radical notion Adams despised. He would tolerate slavery where it existed but he would fight its expansion as well as any attempt to prevent the free expression of those who abhorred the institution. So when he finally raised his voice in defense of the right of petition he not surprisingly gained the reputation of a fierce and dedicated enemy of slavery.

The fight began in the House of Representatives on December 16, 1835, with the presentation of the first abolition petition. Representative James H. Hammond of South Carolina moved that it not be received. The Speaker, James K. Polk of Tennessee, permitted several members to argue in favor of a gag and then shut off further debate. Adams rose and asked to be heard. His intention was obvious. When his opponents tried to prevent him from speaking he cried out, "Am I gagged, or am I not?" A long and increasingly vicious argument ensued that lasted six weeks. The anger and verbal fury elicited in the debate so alarmed a number of congressmen that they armed themselves with knives when they entered the chamber.

And Adams led the fight. In one speech he admitted his belief that the Constitution forbade any interference with slavery in the states but then he modified it by declaring that if armed conflict resulted Congress could use its war powers to deal "with the institution of slavery in every way."

He was particularly determined to protect the right of petition. One of the petitions asked Congress to protect northern citizens going to the South from "danger to their lives." It was followed by a motion to lay it on the table, whereupon JQA rose and said, "In another part of the Capitol it had been threatened that if a Northern abolitionist should go to North Carolina and utter a principle of the Declaration of Independence—." At that point he was interrupted with cries of "Order! Order!" He stood at his place and waited until the tumult subsided "and then resumed, 'that if they could catch him they would hang him.'" Now the shouts of "Order!" became deafening.

His determination to defend the right of petition led the House to form a special committee under the chairmanship of Representative Henry L. Pinckney of South Carolina to examine the question and bring back a report. What the committee produced on May 18, 1836, was the so-called gag resolution, which stated that "all petitions, memorials, resolutions, propositions or papers relating in any way or to any extent whatever to the subject of slavery or the abolition of slavery shall, without being printed or referred, be laid upon the table and that no further action whatever shall be had thereon." There were two other resolutions. The first stated that Congress had no power over slavery in the states. It was adopted by a vote of 182 to 9, Adams voting against it. The second held that interference with slavery in the District of Columbia was inexpedient. It passed 132 to 45, Adams abstaining. On the gag resolution, when his name was called, Adams shouted out, "I hold the resolution to be a direct violation of the Constitution of the United States, of the rules of this House, and of the rights of my constituents." Even so it passed on May 26 by a vote of 117 to 68.

Adams was in his element. He had found a cause worthy of his dedication and talents. He was fighting for a principle that transcended such things as banks and tariffs and internal improvements. And he gloried in the national and international attention he attracted. He was seen as a fighter for freedom who battled against the forces of repression and tyranny. With this weapon he was able to pay back many of the "skunks" who had sullied his character over the years. With this weapon Old Man Eloquent pilloried the slavocracy and all those who protected or defended it. Many times he was shrill, argumentative, caustic, and quarrelsome. Several times he got into a shouting match with the Speaker or other members of the House. Sharp, quick, and unrelenting, he frequently maneuvered southerners into untenable positions. At times he was so impassioned, so mischievous, so wild in his denunciations that even his friends thought he had lost his mind. Jackson certainly did. "He must be demented, if not, then he is the most reckless and depraved man living," the Hero wrote. He belongs in a hospital, Jackson raged. Many southern congressmen called Adams "the Madman from Massachusetts."

With each new session of Congress Adams renewed his attack on the gag resolution. The Speaker had ruled that the Pinckney resolutions expired at the close of the last session and had to be reinstated when Congress reassembled. That ruling gave Adams the opportunity before the House was fully organized to launch three-hour diatribes about the sanctity of petition and the need to defend the Constitution. Any attempt to stop him led to an uproar with Adams "snarling and quarreling," shouting and bickering in a most "uncivilized" manner. "Expel him! Expel him!" frequently rent the air.

The debates, year after year, turned Adams into a hero for many ordinary citizens. He had now achieved a degree of popularity that had eluded him his entire life. In Cincinnati, for example, the advocates of abolition raised a banner across Sixth Street: "John Quincy Adams, the Defender of the Rights of Man." Obviously he had made a mark and taken a stand on an issue that he knew would be remembered long after his death.

The question of slavery provoked additional dissension when Texas won its independence from Mexico in 1836 and petitioned for annexation by the United States as a slave territory. Mexico had freed its slaves, and Texas, according to Adams, now wished to safeguard and perpetuate slavery by entering the Union. So he jumped into the lead in opposing admission. On May 25, 1836, he expressed his views in an hour-long speech frequently punctuated by catcalls from other members and from the galleries. Still, he drove ahead. He mocked the irony of placing the United States in the position of thwarting freedom and strengthening oppression by admitting Texas. Furthermore, such a move could provoke war with Mexico, he argued, and might involve Great Britain, which had freed its slaves and had taken the lead among European nations in advocating emancipation. France might intervene as well. Was the nation prepared to face possible combat against three powerful foes, he asked. Worse, the Indians might rise up against the country and incite a slave insurrection. All these horrors could result from annexation, he contended.

Why do it? "Are you not large and unwieldy enough already? Do not two millions of square miles cover surface enough for the insatiate capacity of your land-jobbers? . . . Have you not Indians enough to expel from the land of their fathers' sepulchers, and to exterminate?"

A powerful speech, and it raised John Quincy Adams even higher in the estimation of abolitionists. Not that he believed they could make a difference. If ever slavery is to be abolished in this country, he declared, it would come through either civil war or the consent of the slave owners, certainly not by the actions of abolitionists. He doubted whether emancipation would happen in his lifetime but when it did come it could very well "be preceded by convulsions and revolutions in the moral, political, and physical world, from which I turn away my eyes to more cheering contemplations." For Adams the best he could hope for was the containment of slavery rather than its abolition. A bloody civil war would constitute a national disaster, he argued, and could lead to further "convulsions."

Of the more than one hundred thousand petitions flooding Congress about slavery, Adams singled out several written by associations of women, including one from the ladies of Fredericksburg, and attempted to read them. It always helped to demonstrate female opposition to any measure. Whereupon John Mercer Patton of Virginia claimed the floor and declared that he was raised in Fredericksburg and that not a name of a respectable woman could he recognize on the petition in question, except a mulatto of "infamous" character. The rest were all free Negroes or mulattoes.

"The honorable gentleman," rumbled Adams in response, "makes it a crime because I presented a petition which he affirms to be from colored women, which women were of infamous character, as the honorable gentleman says—prostitutes, I think the gentleman said."

"I did not say they were prostitutes."

"I thought the honorable gentleman had said they were 'infamous.'" Even so, were not the humblest members of a free society permitted to beg for mercy and exercise the "sacred right of petition"?

"I have not said that I know these women," Patton continued to protest.

What an opening!—and Adams quickly seized it. "I am glad to hear the honorable gentleman disclaim any knowledge of them," he replied with a straight face, "for I had been going to ask, if they were infamous women, then who is it that had made them infamous? Not their color, I believe, but their masters! I have heard it said in proof of that fact, and I am inclined to believe it is the case, that in the South there existed great resemblances between the progeny of the colored people and the white men who claim possession of them. Thus, perhaps, the charges of infamous might be retorted on those who made it, as originating from themselves."

The House erupted—or, as the *Register of Debates* in Congress sedately reported, "Great agitation in the House." Old Man Eloquent had landed a solid blow at the slavocracy, driving southerners to near frenzy.

Although President Jackson favored annexation he recognized the danger of inciting the abolitionists to civil unrest. Moreover, he feared for the election to the presidency of his chosen successor, Martin Van Buren, and the likelihood of war with Mexico. He therefore put off proposing annexation and at the behest of

Congress in late February and early March 1837 he formally recognized Texas independence by nominating a chargé d'affaires who was confirmed during the final hours of his administration.

To find solace from these nerve-wracking episodes in the House, Adams sometimes spoke of the need to turn his mind to more "cheering contemplations." When he did so he might very well have thought about the recent gift of James Smithson, the illegitimate son of the Duke of Northumberland, who had left his entire estate of half a million dollars in gold to the United States for "an establishment for the increase and diffusion of knowledge," the sort of thing Adams had proposed as president. In the House JQA suggested that a special committee be formed to decide how the money should be spent. The motion was approved, and of course, as its sponsor, he was automatically appointed its chairman.

Now he had a second fight on his hands: keep the bequest from being "wasted upon hungry and worthless political jackals." He managed to defeat every demand that the money be assigned to some personal and individual project. He also opposed the creation of a university because the money was intended for the public, he contended, not the elite few. Of course he too had a pet scheme and that was the establishment of an astronomical observatory, what his opponents had once called "lighthouses of the skies." He spent many hours laboring over how to use the gift and frequently met with President Van Buren and his cabinet to discuss the various proposals put forward. It took ten long years to find the answer: the establishment of the Smithsonian Institution. By that time Adams had been replaced as chairman of the committee; still he deserves as much credit as anyone else for the creation of this magnificent addition to American life and culture. No one, says Samuel Flagg Bemis, did more than he to keep it out of politics, and no one since Benjamin Franklin accomplished as much in advancing the cause of science in America.

With all the battles he waged during his years as a congressman he became very adept at maneuvering around, over, and between the rules of the House in order to speak up for what he believed were the great moral values this country represented. On slavery and freedom of speech he had become more and more vehement and courageous, but on other issues dealing with racial equality, gender, ethnicity, and religious tolerance he was less heroic. Interracial marriage he insisted was "contrary to the laws of nature." He also opposed women's suffrage and frequently made sarcastic remarks about Jews and Roman Catholics. He invariably stood midway between opposing views of some of the most important social, cultural, and political issues of the Jacksonian age. Perhaps more than anyone else of his generation John Quincy Adams represented the thinking, opinions, and attitudes of the vast majority of American citizens—just like his father before him. Unfortunately it took another century before that fact received the recognition it so rightly deserved.

12

Victory!

John Quincy Adams's presidency may have been a disaster—historians who regularly run polls on the presidents usually list him as "below average"—but everything else in his public life added distinction to this nation's illustrious history. He envisioned the United States as a continental power and helped achieve it. He conceived and formulated one of this country's most basic doctrines on foreign policy. And, during his final years, he devoted himself to protecting fundamental human rights.

One prime example of his concern for human rights involved his efforts in winning the freedom of thirty-nine African captives aboard the slave schooner *Amistad*. Intended as slaves to work the plantations in Cuba they were being transported on a Spanish vessel when, under the leadership of Cinqué, they rebelled, killing the captain and most of the crew. The few surviving sailors were directed to sail for Africa but managed to deceive the Africans and head up the Atlantic coast where the ship was captured off Long Island by a U.S. warship in August 1839 and taken to New London, Connecticut.

Spanish authorities demanded the immediate return of the ship and the Africans, denying American jurisdiction in the matter. But the question at issue was whether the captives were slaves or freemen. Abolitionists and others banded together to protect the prisoners, provide legal assistance, and prevent their return. In a series of decisions both the district and circuit federal U.S. courts sided with the Africans, declaring they were not property and had been unlawfully seized. But the Van Buren administration, concerned about southern reaction to the decisions in an election year, appealed the case to the Supreme Court.

Outraged by the response of the government, aware that the court was heavily weighted in favor of the proslavery position since all but two of the justices (Joseph Story and Smith Thompson) had been appointed by Jackson and Van Buren, and always seeking revenge for the Little Magician's leading role in wrecking his administration, Adams offered his legal services to Lewis Tappan, a wealthy abolitionist who had been instrumental in organizing the defense of the captives. In offering his services Old Man Eloquent did not expect to plead the case because of his limitations as an advocate and because he had not appeared before the high court since 1809. Tappan accepted his offer but ardently appealed to Adams to argue the case with Roger Baldwin, the Connecticut attorney who had guided it through the lower courts. "I am too old," Adams responded, "too oppressed by my duties in the House of Representatives, too inexperienced after a lapse of thirty years in the forms and technicalities of arguments before the Supreme Court." What Tappan asked was really impossible. "But I will cheerfully do what I have hitherto offered, that is, to give any assistance with counsel and advice to Mr. Baldwin."

That was not good enough. Tappan and his abolitionist friends demanded more. "It is a case of life and death, for these unfortunate men," they insisted.

The old man relented. "By the blessing of God, I will argue the case before the Supreme Court," he said.

Actually, Adams was a skillful researcher who knew how to probe and analyze documents to provide essential evidence. Once he accepted the assignment he set to work with his usual diligence and concentration, requesting all the relevant documents held by the government dealing with the *Amistad* matter, some of which had to be virtually pried loose from the state department.

Hardly a week before the Van Buren administration ended, the *Amistad* case opened the Supreme Court's February term. The government's argument against the captives was straightforward and seemingly airtight. In several treaties, including the Adams-Onís Treaty of 1819, Spain and the United States had agreed to respect one another's property, which naturally included slaves since both nations recognized them as property. The Africans were "slaves," according to the government, and therefore must be handed over to the Spanish authorities for deportation.

In response Baldwin argued against the government's interference. The case was purely a local matter. The captives were freemen, he contended, not slaves, and simply acted in self-defense by fighting for their rights and seizing control of the ship to get back home.

Adams followed and leveled a blistering attack on the Van Buren administration and the Spanish government for daring to accuse these captives of piracy and theft. And his pleading graphically demonstrated how much his speaking skills had been honed by virtue of his many verbal brawls on the floor of the House of Representatives. Actually, he asked, who were the real thieves and pirates? Certainly not Cinqué and his associates. The criminals in this case were the captain and crew of the *Amistad*, who illegally seized these men and sought to enslave them. Then he pointed to a copy of the Declaration of Independence hanging on the wall. "The moment you come to the Declaration of Independence, that every man has a right to life and liberty, as an inalienable right, this case is decided. I ask nothing more on behalf of these unfortunate men, than this Declaration." He ended by dismissing the argument concerning maritime law and the rights of property. His entire presentation was a plea for human rights.

It was a splendid presentation, and he scored one telling point after another. Justice Joseph Story, one of the two non-Jacksonian appointees, marveled at what he had heard. "Extraordinary," he exclaimed. "Extraordinary for its power and its bitter sarcasm, and its dealing with topics far beyond the record and points of discussion."

A week later the court rendered its decision, which was read by Story. The majority, including Chief Justice Roger B. Taney, a slaveholder, declared the Africans freemen and dismissed as immaterial the treaties involving slave property. Only Justice Henry Baldwin dissented.

Tappan and other members of the defense committee sent Adams their thanks for "valuable services, gratuitously rendered, in rescuing the lives and liberties of our humble clients from the imminent peril to which they were exposed." But he also received a reward that greatly pleased him. It was "a splendidly bound quarto Bible" with an address signed by "Cinque, Kinna and Kale for the thirty-four Mendian Africans of the Amistad."

It was a final defeat for President Van Buren whose administration had been plagued from the beginning by an extended economic depression—the Panic of 1837. He and the entire Democratic party had been trounced the previous fall, 1840, in one of the most non-sensical presidential campaigns in American history. The Whig candidates, William Henry Harrison of Ohio and his running mate, John Tyler of Virginia, won a stunning victory. "Tippecanoe and Tyler, Too," sang the Whigs. "Van, Van is a Used up Man."

With the inauguration of the new administration Adams was regularly invited to White House dinners and invariably Harrison asked him to offer the first toast. After all he had advanced Harrison's career by appointing him to a diplomatic post some fifteen-odd years earlier. But a month later the president died unexpectedly and Vice President Tyler, a former Democrat who had deserted to the Whig party over the nullification controversy, became the chief executive. As it turned out Tyler still retained many Jacksonian precepts, especially regarding the national bank and protective tariffs.

Adams was stunned by this unforeseen tragedy. He rejected Tyler's right to assume the full powers of the presidency. To do so, he said, would violate the Constitution. Tyler was nothing but a "slave breeder" and a dishonest one at that. But Tyler achieved a notable constitutional victory in insisting on his right to full presidential powers, a victory finally made explicit 125 years later with the passage of the 25th Amendment.

When the new Whig-controlled Congress convened, Adams was rewarded by being named chairman of the Foreign Relations Committee, the post he had desired since he began his congressional career. Not that it kept him quiet. If anything, it encouraged him to greater efforts to kill the gag rule. Frequently his outbursts became so quarrelsome that he seemed out of control. At one point he had the effrontery to present a petition from a group in Massachusetts who asked Congress to adopt measures by which the United States could be "peaceably" dissolved. Adams asked that it be referred to a committee with instructions to report a reply stating the reasons the petition should be denied.

And that did it. Southerners howled their horror. "I demand," cried one, "that you shut the mouth of that old harlequin." They were determined to censure him for even hinting at dismembering the Union, and a motion to that effect was promptly introduced in the House.

Adams could not have been more delighted. He was now forced to stand "trial" for his beliefs. In reality, he raged, it was a "conspiracy to crush the liberties of the free people of the Union." They "would crucify me if their vote could erect the cross."

Since he was now on "trial," he had the right to defend himself and he used it to launch a long and systematic assault on the "slavocracy." Again he ranted and shouted and called names, names like "beef-witted blunderhead" and "slave monger." He singled out several House members for personal abuse and charged one individual with being "drunk with whiskey and drunk with slavery." He accused another who had recently engaged in a duel with having "his hands and face dripping with the blood of murder." Who could believe that this was the same John Quincy Adams of old, the ex-president and revered statesman?

Finally, after a prolonged indictment of the "peculiar institution" and its defenders, even he recognized that these antics had gotten out of hand. "My language is too violent," he admitted, "and must be smoothed down." Red-faced and perspiring, his hands gripping the sides of his desk to hold himself erect, he ended his harangue and allowed the resolution to come to a vote. It was defeated, 105 to 80, on February 4, 1842.

But the "trial" of so distinguished a statesman as ex-president John Quincy Adams publicized to the nation the danger to freedom and justice that all men and women faced if they dared raise their voices against slavery. It marked the beginning of the end of the gag.

Session after session he had kept arguing and fighting to prevent the gag's passage and each year he had been defeated by the "chicanery of moving for the previous question and reconsideration, and laying on the table, and to divide the question, and every species of subterfuge." The strain was beginning to show and sometimes he was so weak and ill that he could barely rise to his feet to speak. Still, he kept at it and with each passing year the vote against him steadily dwindled. Northern Democrats were feeling the pressure of their constituents who believed with Adams that the gag contradicted the most basic concepts on which this nation was founded.

The "conspiracy," as Adams called it, to advance the spread of slavery in the United States became more real when President Tyler and his new secretary of state, John C. Calhoun, succeeded in obtaining a treaty for the annexation of Texas. Signed by representatives of the two countries on April 12, 1844, the treaty admitted Texas as a slave territory and assumed its debts by the United States up to a maximum of $10 million. When the document was submitted to the Senate for ratification—"and with it went the freedom of the human race," moaned Adams—Calhoun made the mistake of sending a letter to the British minister in Washington explaining that the action was meant to protect American slavery from British efforts to win universal emancipation. Calhoun's fumble had the beneficial effect of uniting Whig senators with a number of northern Democrats, who reckoned that "it would be death to them, politically, if they were to vote for the Treaty based on such principles," and together they defeated the treaty "16 yeas to 35 nays," much to Adams's surprise and delight. "I record this vote," he wrote, "as a delivery, I trust, by the special interposition of Almighty God, of my country and of human liberty."

Tyler had hoped his action would provide him a nomination from the Democratic party in the presidential election of 1844. But that party remained loyal to Van Buren until he openly declared his opposition to annexation, whereupon it nominated James Knox Polk of Tennessee, Jackson's protégé. The Democratic platform called for the reannexation of Texas (they insisted that John Quincy Adams "criminally" surrendered it in the Adams-Onís Treaty of

1819) and the reoccupation of Oregon. The platform breathed the spirit of "Manifest Destiny," which declared in the words of John L. O'Sullivan, the editor of *The Democratic Review*, that it "is by the right of manifest destiny" for the United States "to overspread and to possess the whole of the continent which Providence has given us for the development of the great experiment in liberty and federative self government entrusted to us."

The Whigs turned once again to Henry Clay, who also declared his opposition to annexation. But then he waffled on the issue and that, together with the "corrupt bargain" many people still held against him, brought Polk a narrow victory. Adams easily won reelection against both the candidates of the Democratic and Liberty parties. A few times in past elections he had come close to defeat when his antics in Congress caused his constituents to worry about his sanity. But he always managed to escape, and this latest victory, considering his age, gave him immense satisfaction.

When Congress reconvened on December 2, 1844, conditions seemed ripe for an end of the gag rule. Once again Adams, as he had done so many times in the past, proposed that it be rescinded, and this time it was, on December 3, 1844, by a vote of 108 to 80.

Adams exulted. "Blessed, forever blessed, be the name of God," he exclaimed in his diary.

But the victory was short-lived. Capitalizing on Polk's triumph in the presidential election, Tyler proposed a joint resolution of both houses of Congress by which Texas would be admitted into the Union as a slave state and retain its public lands and debt. Despite protests that this procedure violated the Constitution, since the treaty-making power belonged exclusively to the Senate, the resolution passed both houses and Tyler signed it on March 1, 1845. Texas ratified the annexation on July 4 and was admitted as a slave state into the Union on December 29, 1845. "The Constitution is a menstruous rag," a disgusted Adams raged, "and the Union is sinking into a military monarchy, to be rent asunder like the empire of Alexander."

Although he rejected the admission of Texas because of slavery, Adams emphatically supported President Polk's plan to terminate the joint occupation of Oregon with Great Britain and claim the entire Northwest Territory clear up to the 54° 40' parallel, the boundary of Russian Alaska. The Democratic platform in the election of 1844 had included the cry "54° 40' or fight," and presumably Polk now proposed to implement that demand.

Once more Adams's old advocacy of territorial expansion surfaced and since slavery did not exist in Oregon there was no contradiction to his stand against Texas's annexation. He also argued that the United States had a better claim to the territory than the British because of the Lewis and Clark expedition and the Adams-Onís Treaty. But Polk had an even more important objective in mind. He lusted after California with its long coastline and splendid harbors fronting the Pacific Ocean. So he willingly agreed to a treaty with the British on June 18, 1846, to fix the border between the United States and Canada at the forty-ninth parallel—an action JQA approved. Once England had been neutralized he offered to purchase California from Mexico. When the offer was refused Polk ordered General Zachary Taylor to cross the Texas border and advance to the Rio Grande. The Mexican army attacked, sixteen Americans were killed, and Polk asked Congress for a declaration of war.

The action horrified Adams. Not that he opposed war as a general principle. "There are," he declared, "and always have been as long as the race of men has existed, times and occasions of dire necessity for war; and, philosophically speaking, I believed that war was not a corrupter, but rather a purifier, of the moral character of man; that peace was the period of corruption to the human race." But in this case what Polk requested was outright aggression.

Both houses of Congress immediately voted for the declaration and Polk signed it on May 13, 1846. Adams did all he could to rally opposition to the war but he was now nearly seventy-nine years of age and he no longer had the strength to fight as he had over the past decade. He had grown frail and he looked feeble. Sometimes he had to be helped to his seat. But he and a number of other congressmen (mostly from New England) voted against this "most outrageous war," as he called it, even though shouts of "traitors" were repeatedly hurled at them. The declaration of war passed the House by the vote of 117 to 50 with Adams shouting "no" as loudly as possible.

Because of his declining health he spoke less and less during the final congressional sessions of his life. He left the denunciation of the Mexican outrage to others. But when a southerner attempted to compensate the owners of the *Amistad* for their "property" loss he roused himself sufficiently to defeat it. He also voted for the "proviso" offered by David Wilmot, the Democratic Pennsylvania representative, to exclude slavery from any territory obtained from Mexico as a result of the war.

When Andrew Jackson died shortly after Polk's inauguration, Adams did not forget that this so-called hero was also a "murderer, and adulterer, and a profoundly pious presbyterian, who, in the last days of his life, belied and slandered me before the world." JQA never forgot what Jackson had done to him, and he never forgave the "profoundly pious presbyterian."

After returning to Massachusetts following the adjournment of Congress in 1846 he suffered a slight stroke on November 20 that paralyzed his right side for several days and left him mentally confused and speechless. But, to the surprise of his doctors and family, he slowly recovered and after regaining some of his old strength returned to Congress in mid-February. Still, from the moment he suffered the stroke, "I date my decease, and consider myself, for every useful purpose to myself or to my fellow-creatures, dead."

He braved this final session of the Twenty-ninth Congress and returned again to Washington when Congress reconvened on December 6, 1847. By this time his colleagues treated him as something of a relic. Although he continued to weaken each day and found that attending Congress had become a real burden he nonetheless felt duty bound to at least put in an appearance.

With the Mexican War slowly coming to an end a resolution was offered in the House on February 21, 1848, to commend the veterans of the country's recent military victories. Adams voted no, as usual, and when the clerk started to read a tribute to the soldiers the old man struggled to his feet to gain the floor and register a protest. As he rose he suddenly faltered and began to topple but a colleague caught him in time and kept him from collapsing to the floor.

"Mr. Adams is dying!" screamed a voice in the chamber. He was rushed to the Speaker's office but there was nothing that could be done. He struggled to remain conscious, saying, "This is the end of earth, but I am composed." Then he lapsed into a coma and died two days later in the Capitol building at 7:15 P.M. on February 23, 1848.

The funeral ceremonies were held in the House, and the silver-mounted coffin bore an inscription written by Daniel Webster—whom Adams despised—at the request of the Massachusetts delegation to Congress. It read:

JOHN QUINCY ADAMS
BORN
an inhabitant of Massachusetts
July 11, 1767
DIED
A citizen of the United States, in the Capitol of
Washington, February 23, 1848, Having served his country
for half a century, And enjoyed its highest honors.

Adams's biographer Samuel Flagg Bemis says that if the old man looked down from "Olympus" he surely must have been pleased with the inscription, "if not the hand that wrote it."

Just a short time before this last stroke Adams himself assessed his career. "With regard to what is called the wheel of Fortune, my career in life has been, with severe vicissitudes, on the whole highly auspicious."

Indeed. And the respect and admiration Americans had for him and what he accomplished during his lifetime have mounted over the years and will undoubtedly keep mounting into the future. Surely he now feels completely vindicated.

Notes

1: A PRIVILEGED YOUNG MAN

The quotations and arguments in this chapter come from Adams, *Memoirs*, 6: 417–18; 1: 5–6, 7, 8–9; 9: 159, 289; 12: 277; Butterfield, ed., *Adams Family Correspondence*, 1: 167, 252, 384; 2: 177–78, 254, 289–91, 307; 3: 16, 37–38, 92–94, 97, 268, 312; 4: 38–39, 68, 136, 206, 277, 323; 5: 37–38, 86–87, 218, 220–21, 242, 273–74, 341; Bemis, *JQA*, 1: 8, 9, 11; Nagel, *JQA*, pp. 12, 31; Adams, ed., *Letters of Mrs Adams*, pp. 95–96, 111–16, 126–27, 152–54, 424–25; Hecht, *JQA*, p. 24; Ford, ed., *Writings of JQA*, 1: 1–2 n., 7–10, 17–20.

2: FINDING A CAREER

The quotations and arguments in this chapter come from Adams, *Memoirs*, 1: 90, 150–51, 188, 195, 199–200; Nagel, *JQA*, pp. 45, 67–69, 76, 81, 100; Bemis, *JQA*, 1: 80, 82; Ford, ed., *Writings of JQA*, 1: 29, 65–110, 135–46, 192, 202, 210–14; 2: 18–20, 46–47, 101–06, 173–75.

3: FROM FEDERALIST TO REPUBLICAN

The quotations in this chapter come from Nagel, *JQA*, pp. 135, 174, 178, 180, 198, 200, 203, 218–19; Hecht, *JQA*, p. 146; Parsons, *JQA*, pp. 79, 90–91, 103, 111–13, 120, 123; Bemis, *JQA*, 1: 129, 196, 241; Adams, *Memoirs*, 2: 51, 656, 657–58; 3: 21, 32, 566; Ford, ed., *Writings of JQA*, 5: 236, 237, 239; Geheimes Staatsarchiv Preussischer Kulturbesitz, pp. 4, 6.

4: SECRETARY OF STATE

The quotations in this chapter come from Ford, ed., *Writings of JQA*, 6: 319ff; *ASPFR*, 4: 375–78, 526–31; Monroe to Jackson, December 28, 1818, Monroe Papers; Adams, *Memoirs*, 4: 105–6, 111, 144; 5: 252–53; 6: 104, 178–80; 12: 78, 218; Lewis, *JQA*, p. 86; Bemis, *JQA*, 1: 326, 340, 356, 375–77, 384, 390; Richardson, *Messages of the Presidents*, 1: 761–63.

5: THE ELECTION OF 1824–25

The quotations in this chapter come from Adams, *Memoirs*, 6: 323–24; 5: 298; Parsons, *JQA*, pp. 155, 165, 171; Remini, *Clay*, pp. 240–41, 246, 253–58, 260–68; Nagel, *JQA*, pp. 294, 296.

6: "THE PERILOUS EXPERIMENT"

The quotations in this chapter come from Adams, *Memoirs*, 6: 518; 7: 28, 58–64; 12: 255; Richardson, *Messages of the Presidents*, 2: 866–68, 872, 879, 882; Remini, *Jackson*, 2: 110–11, 113–15; *Register of Debates*, 19th Congress, 1st Session, pp. 142–43, 154–74, 234–62, 398–404; Hargreaves, *Presidency of JQA*, pp. 173–79, 198.

7: INDIAN REMOVAL

The quotations in this chapter come from Adams, *Memoirs*, 7: 3, 66, 76, 87, 90–92, 106, 113, 219, 220, 411; Remini, *Election of Andrew Jackson*, pp. 102–3; Nagel, *JQA*, p. 304; Bemis, *JQA*, 2: 80, 86, 87; Green, *Indian Removal*, pp. 89, 102–3, 105, 113, 119, 122–23, 127; Richardson, *Messages of the Presidents*, 2: 960–61; *ASPIA*, 2: 869–72.

8: DIPLOMATIC SUCCESSES AND FAILURES

The quotations in this chapter come from Adams, *Memoirs*, 7: 175, 240, 242, 263, 361, 328; 6: 539; Parsons, *JQA*, pp. 183–84; Remini, *Clay*, pp. 290, 307–10, 315; Hargreaves, *Presidency of JQA*, pp. 82–84.

9: THE TARIFF OF ABOMINATIONS

The quotations in this chapter come from Adams, *Memoirs*, 7: 103, 342, 366–67, 402, 472, 531, 534; 8: 25; Remini, *Clay*, pp. 316–17, 323; Remini, *Election of Andrew Jackson*, pp. 168, 172–73, 174, 178.

10: "SKUNKS OF PARTY SLANDER"

The quotations in this chapter come from Adams, *Memoirs*, 10: 47, 49, 76, 89; 7: 415–16, 431, 477; Remini, *Election of Andrew Jackson*, pp. 79, 102–5, 107, 110, 115–16, 118, 123, 126, 131–32, 134, 139–40, 144, 150, 155, 181; Remini, *Jackson*, p. 13.

11: CONGRESSMAN JOHN QUINCY ADAMS

The quotations in this chapter come from Adams, *Memoirs*, 8: 247; 9: 283, 287–88, 339; 11: 419; 12: 93, 136; Parsons, *JQA*, 210–11, 213, 223, 225, 231, 233; Nagel, *JQA*, 330, 335, 343, 348, 353, 364, 357; *Register of Debates*, 24th Congress, 1st Session, pp. 404ff, 1103–8, 1136–71, 1556–98, 1721–35; Bemis, *JQA*, 2: 344, 346, 523.

12: VICTORY!

The quotations in this chapter come from Adams, *Memoirs*, 9: 294; 11: 29, 67–70, 81, 98–99, 521; 12: 14, 49, 115–16, 171, 206, 218–19, 240, 255, 279; Bemis, *JQA*, 2: 399–400, 539; Parsons, *JQA*, pp. 239, 264, 266; *Congressional Globe*, 27th Congress, 2nd Session, pp. 157–67, 207; Nagel, *JQA*, 385–86, 403, 405, 413; Schlesinger, *Cycles of American History*, p. 344.

Milestones

1767 Born in Braintree (later Quincy), Massachusetts
1774 Intolerable Acts
1776 Declaration of Independence
1778–81 Educated in Europe
1781 Mission to St. Petersburg
      Lord Cornwallis surrenders at Yorktown
1783 Returns to Paris with his father
      Treaty of Paris signed ending the American Revolution
1785 Returns to the United States
1786 Enters Harvard University
1787 Graduates Harvard
1787–88 Constitution written and adopted
1787–90 Studies law
1789 George Washington elected president
1790 Sworn in as attorney
1791 Publishes "Letters of Publicola"
1793–94 Writes newspaper articles defending President Washington
      and policy of neutrality
1794 Appointed minister resident to the Netherlands
1796 John Adams elected president
1797 Appointed minister plenipotentiary to Prussia
      Marries Louisa Catherine Johnson
1799 Napoleon Bonaparte assumes control of France
1800 Thomas Jefferson elected president
1801 Son George Washington Adams born
      Recalled to United States
1802 Elected to Massachusetts legislature
      Elected to U.S. Senate

1803   Louisiana purchased from France
       Son John Adams II born
1803–15   Resumption of the Napoleonic Wars
1806   Appointed Boylston Professor at Harvard
1807   Son Charles Francis Adams born
1808   Resigns Senate seat
       James Madison elected president
1809   Appointed minister to Russia
1811   Daughter Louisa Catherine born
1812   United States declares war against Great Britain
       Daughter Louisa dies
1814   Appointed to head peace commission
       Signs Treaty of Ghent ending War of 1812
1815   Battle of New Orleans
       Peace treaty ratified by Senate
1816   James Monroe elected president
1817   Appointed secretary of state
1818   Mother dies
1819   Negotiates Adams-Onís Treaty
1823   Conceives Monroe Doctrine
1825   Elected president
       Inaugurated president
       Signs Treaty of Indian Springs
       Nominates ministers to Panama Congress
1826   Approves Treaty of Washington
       Father dies
1827   Attempts to purchase Texas
       Imposes trade restrictions with West Indies
1828   Signs Tariff of Abominations
       Defeated for reelection
       Andrew Jackson elected president
1829   Son George commits suicide
1830   Elected to Congress
1832   President Jackson vetoes bank bill
       South Carolina nullifies tariff
1833   Runs for governor of Massachusetts and then withdraws
1834   Son John II dies
1835–44   Fights gag resolution
1836   Gag resolution passed
       Opposes Texas annexation
       Martin Van Buren elected president
1840   William Henry Harrison elected president
1841   Argues *Amistad* case before Supreme Court
1842   Censure of Adams in House of Representatives defeated

1844   James Knox Polk elected president
       Gag resolution rescinded
1845   Texas annexed
1846   United States declares war against Mexico
1848   Dies in Capitol

Bibliography

Adams, Charles Francis, ed. *Letters of John Adams*. Boston, 1841.
_____. *Letters of Mrs. Adams, the Wife of John Adams*. Boston, 1841.
_____. *Memoirs of John Quincy Adams, Comprising Portions of his Diary from 1795 to 1848*. 12 vols. Philadelphia, 1874–77.
Adams, John Quincy. *Argument of John Quincy Adams Before the Supreme Court of the United States in the Case of the United States vs. Cinque and other Africans*. New York, 1841.
_____. *Letters on Silesia*. London, 1804.
American State Papers, Foreign Relations (ASPFR). Washington, D.C., 1832–59.
American State Papers, Indian Affairs (ASPIA). Washington, D.C., 1832–59.
Bemis, Samuel Flagg. *John Quincy Adams and the Foundations of American Foreign Policy*. New York, 1949.
_____. *John Quincy Adams and the Union*. New York, 1956.
Butterfield, Lyman H., ed. *Adams Family Correspondence*. Cambridge, 1963–93.
_____. *Diary and Autobiography of John Adams*. New York, 1964.
Congressional Globe, 1836–48.
East, Robert. *John Quincy Adams: The Critical Years, 1785–94*. New York, 1962.
Ford, Worthington C., ed. *Writings of John Quincy Adams*. 7 vols. New York, 1913–17.
Geheimes Staatsarchiv Preussischer Kulturbesitz, Berlin. R. xi, m. 21.a, Amerika 2.5, 1797–1801.
Green, Michael D. *The Politics of Indian Removal: Creek Government and Society in Crisis*. Lincoln, Nebr., 1982.
Hargreaves, Mary W. M. *The Presidency of John Quincy Adams*. Lawrence, Kans., 1985.

Hecht, Marie B. *John Quincy Adams: A Personal History of an Independent Man*. New York, 1972.

Hopkins, James F. et al., eds. *The Papers of Henry Clay*. 10 vols and supplement. Lexington, Ky., 1959–92.

Howe, Daniel Walker. *The Political Culture of the American Whigs*. Chicago, 1979.

Lewis, James E. Jr. *John Quincy Adams: Policymaker for the Union*. Wilmington, Del., 2001.

Lipsky, George A. *John Quincy Adams: His Theory and Ideas*. New York, 1950.

May, Ernest. *The Making of the Monroe Doctrine*. Cambridge, Mass., 1975.

McCullough, David. *John Adams*. New York, 2001.

Miller, William Lee. *Arguing About Slavery: The Great Battle in the United States Congress*. New York, 1996.

Monroe, James. James Monroe Papers. New York Public Library, Manuscript Division, 1989.

Nagel, Paul C. *The Adams Women: Abigail and Louisa Adams, Their Sisters and Daughters*. New York, 1987.

_____. *Descent from Glory: Four Generations of the John Adams Family*. New York, 1983.

_____. *John Quincy Adams: A Public Life, a Private Life*. New York, 1997.

Nevins, Allan, ed. *The Diary of John Quincy Adams*. New York, 1928.

Parsons, Lynn Hudson. *John Quincy Adams*. Madison, Wis., 1998.

Register of Debates in Congress. 1835–36.

Remini, Robert V. *Election of Andrew Jackson*. New York, 1963.

_____. *Andrew Jackson*. New York, 1966.

_____. *Andrew Jackson and the Course of American Freedom, 1822–1832*. New York, 1981.

_____. *Andrew Jackson and the Course of American Democracy, 1833–1845*. New York, 1984.

_____. *Henry Clay: Statesman for the Union*. New York, 1991.

Richards, Leonard L. *The Life and Times of Congressman John Quincy Adams*. New York, 1986.

Richardson, James, ed. *Compilation of the Messages and Papers of the Presidents, 1789–1908*. New York, 1908.

Russell, Greg. *John Quincy Adams and the Public Virtues of Diplomacy*. Columbia, Mo., 1995.

Schlesinger, Arthur M., Jr. *The Age of Jackson*. Boston, 1945.

_____. *The Cycles of American History*. Boston, 1986.

_____, ed. *History of American Presidential Elections*. Vol. 1. New York, 1971.

Weeks, William. *John Quincy Adams and American Global Empire*. Lexington, Ky., 1992.

Index

abolition, 137–45
Adams, Abigail (sister), 2, 16, 33
Adams, Abigail Baxter, 1
Adams, Abigail Brown Brooks,
    (daughter-in-law) 131
Adams, Abigail Smith (mother), 2, 3,
    6, 35, 49; dies, 54; as domineering
    mother, 3–4, 6, 7–9, 10, 11,
    12–13, 15, 37, 39, 40, 54; joins
    husband in Europe, 16; opposes
    JQA's marriage plans, 21, 27–28
Adams, Charles (brother), 2, 7, 9, 10,
    33
Adams, Charles Francis (son), 1, 8,
    40, 62, 88, 89, 119, 130, 131,
    135, 138
Adams, George Washington (son), 1,
    32, 40, 47, 89, 117–18, 130–31
Adams, Hannah Bass, 1
Adams, Henry, 1
Adams, John Sr., 1,
Adams, John (father), 1, 49, 52; and
    American Revolution, 5;
    appointed minister, 5–6, 17;
    appoints JQA minister to Prussia
    and recalls him, 29, 32; concludes
    peace treaty, 15; congratulates
    JQA on presidential election, 73;
    and Declaration of Independence,
    5; defeated for reelection, 32;
    diplomatic successes, 14, 16; dies,

89–90; elected president, 29;
    elected vice president, 20;
    influence on JQA, 4–5, 8, 10, 13;
    meets Louisa, 33; prevents war
    with France, 31
Adams II, John (son), 1, 40, 47, 62,
    89, 117–18, 130, 131, 135
Adams, John Quincy: admitted to
    law practice, 21; admitted to Phi
    Beta Kappa, 19–20; appearance,
    13, 15, 16, 30; appointed Boylston
    Professor, 37–38; appointed
    minister to England, 47;
    appointed minister to Portugal,
    28; appointed minister to Prussia,
    29; appointed minister to Russia,
    40; appointed minister resident in
    the Netherlands, 24; appointed
    secretary of state, 48–49; appoints
    Clay to cabinet, 73–74, 75; as
    expansionist, 58–59, 153; as
    Federalist, 23; as husband, 62; as
    nationalist, 57–58, 75, 78–81; as
    parent, 62, 89; as secretary of
    state, 50–61; attends Republican
    meetings, 38–39; attends Harvard,
    19–20; attends University of
    Leyden, 10; attitude toward
    mother, 10, 11, 12, 21; and bank
    war, 133–34; born, 2; career in
    Congress, 35–39, 132–55; censure

Adams, John Quincy (*continued*)
defeated, 150; children born to,
32, 35, 38, 43; children die, 43,
132, 135; courts electoral vote,
71–72; defends Jackson, 55; dies,
154–55; diplomatic
achievements, 50–61; dislike of
law, 3, 20; domestic policy, 44, 79;
early political activities, 23;
education, 4–6, 10, 19–20; elected
to Congress, 35, 131–32; elected
president, 72; elected to state
senate, 34; elected to U.S. Senate,
35; and election of 1824–25,
63–72; and election of 1828,
119–29; electioneers, 65–66, 102;
establishes law practice, 33;
favorite recreations, 50–51, 77;
favors Louisiana Purchase, 36; and
first message to Congress, 78–81;
and Florida treaty, 56; foreign
policy, 44, 57–58, 78–79; guilt
complex, 5, 117, 131; heads peace
commission, 43–47; and human
rights, 146–55; illnesses, 22,
154–55; and Indian removal,
89–100; intellectual strengths, 7,
10, 12, 13, 14–15, 16, 18, 19;
interests in arts, literature and
science, 3, 6, 15, 16, 17, 18, 30;
keeps diary, 8–9, 15; leads fight
against gag, 137–45; and life in
the White House, 77, 88–89; love
of theater and music, 6, 18, 19,
30; love for Mary Frazier, 20–22;
marries Louisa Johnson, 30; meets
and proposes to Louisa Johnson,
26, 27; and Monroe Doctrine,
57–61, 146; negotiates acquisition
of Florida, 54–56, 146; negotiates
fisheries and boundary questions,
52–53; nicknames, 123, 136;
nominated for president, 67;
opinion of Jackson, 90, 128, 135,
139, 154; opposes Jackson
administration, 133–34, 137;
opposes 12th Amendment, 37;
and patronage, 76–77, 101–2,
109–10; personality and
character, 22, 45, 47, 64, 90, 102,
117, 128, 131, 132, 135, 141,
150; pleads before Supreme

Court, 40, 147–48; popularity,
141; and presidential election, 63,
65–66, 118–19, 123; recalled
from Prussia, 32; relations with
father, 15, 16; and religion, 3–4,
43, 121, 128, 129, 131,132;
resigns senate seat, 39; serves as
father's secretary, 13; and slavery,
137, 145; studies law, 20; supports
internal improvements, 79–81,
86, 135; tariffs, 112–16, 133, 134;
trips abroad, 6, 9, 25; views on
abolitionists, 145; views
on government, 22, 57–58,
64, 79–81, 101; views on
marriage, 20, 42; views on
neutrality, 44, 57–58; views on
politics and electioneering, 64,
66, 72, 122–24; views on public
land policy, 86–87; views on
religion, 43; views on war and
peace, 153, views on women's
suffrage 145; writings, 22, 23,
32, 51
Adams, Jr., Joseph, 1
Adams, Sr., Joseph, 1
Adams, Louisa Catherine (daughter),
42, 43
Adams, Louisa Catherine Johnson
(wife), accepts JQA's marriage
proposal, 27; characteristics, 28,
29, 30, 130; children born to, 32,
35, 38, 42; criticized in election,
119; described, 26–27, 30; and
life in White House, 130; as
hostess, 30, 62, 65, 70; marries
JQA, 30; meets in-laws, 33; meets
JQA, 26–27; quarrels with JQA,
40, 41, 117–18; suffers
miscarriages, 31
Adams, Susanna (sister), 1
Adams, Thomas Boylston (brother),
1, 2, 25, 29, 30, 135
Adams, Dr. William, 45–47
Adams-Onís Treaty, 56, 57, 102–3,
148, 151–52, 153
Alexander I, Czar, 40–43, 53, 59–60,
118–19
Alien and Sedition Acts, 32
Ambrister, Robert, 54, 56
American System, 81, 112
Amistad, 146–49, 154

Anderson, Richard C., 82
Andover Academy, 7
Andrews, Major Timothy P., 93
Anti-Masonry, 125–26, 133, 135, 137
Arbuthnot, Alexander, 54, 56
Argentina, 57
Aroostook War, 104
Articles of Confederation, 17, 20
Astor, John Jacob, 50, 52
Austin, Moses, 103
Austin, Stephen F., 103
Austria, 11, 45, 104

Baldwin, Abraham, 36
Baldwin, Henry, 148
Baldwin, Roger, 147
Barbour, James, 76, 93–94, 95–99
Bayard, James A., 36, 43, 44
Bemis, Samuel Flagg, 30, 48, 50, 51,
  56, 61, 144, 155
Benton, Thomas Hart, 83, 88–89,
  115, 124
Berrien, John M., 83
Biddle, Nicholas, 133
Binns, John, 124–25
Bolivar, Simón, 83
Bonaparte, Napoleon, 31, 42–45,
  47–48
Boylston, Nicholas, 37
Boylston, Susannah, 7
Breckinridge, John, 36
British West Indies, 104–8
Brown, James, 76
Bunker Hill, 2, 102
Burr, Aaron, 36, 37, 125
Butler, Pierce, 36

Calhoun, John C., 55, 63, 65, 67, 68,
  75, 91, 110, 116, 125, 135, 139,
  151
California, 153
Campbell, Duncan G., 91, 92
Canada, 103–4
Cañaz, Antonio José, 104
Canning, George, 48, 59–60, 105
Canning, Stratford, 58–59
Cass, Lewis, 96
Castlereagh, Lord, 44, 48, 52
Catherine the Great, 11
Chesapeake, USS, 38
Chile, 57
Cinqué, 146–49

Clay, Henry: and American System,
  81, 112; and bank war, 133–34;
  and "corrupt bargain" charge,
  73–74, 118, 152; and election of
  1828, 121, 124, 126; appointed
  secretary of state, 73–74, 76; as
  JQA's rival, 49, 57; as presidential
  contender, 64, 68, 133, 152; as
  peace commissioner, 44–47;
  attacked, 108, 121; dispenses
  patronage, 101–2, 110; and
  foreign affairs, 82–83, 102–3,
  104–8; and Indian treaty
  abrogation, 98; opinion of Indian
  tribes, 95–96; and Tariff of 1828,
  114; and Tariff of 1833, 134
Clinton, De Witt, 36, 50
Clinton, George, 37, 39
Cobb, Howell, 96
Colombia, 57, 77, 102, 115
Constitution, U.S., 20, 29, 80, 90,
  136, 137, 139, 140–41, 152
Convention of 1818, 53–54
Cook, Daniel, 72–73
Cooper, Thomas, 112
Copley, John Singleton, 30
Cornwallis, Lord, 14
Cranch, Mary, 40
Cranch, Richard, 40
Crawford, William H., 55, 63, 65,
  66–67, 68, 88, 135, 139
Creek Indians, 91–100
Creek National Council, 97, 98
Crowell, Colonel John, 92, 93, 95
Cuba, 102

Dana, Francis, 7, 11, 18
Davis, John, 135
Deane, Silas, 5
Declaration of Independence, 5, 148
Democratic party, 84, 112, 114–16,
  118–29, 136, 138–39, 151–52
Denmark, 11, 14, 42, 104
Dickinson, Charles, 124
Dolph, Eliza, 130–31
Dudley, Lord, 107

Eaton, John H., 65, 115
Election of 1824–25, 1, 62–74
Election of 1828, 117–29
Election of 1832, 133
Election of 1836, 143–44

Election of 1840, 149
Election of 1844, 151–52
Era of Good Feelings, 77–78
Erie Canal, 112
Erving, George W., 56
Essex Junto, 35
Eustis, Dr. William, 34
Everett, Alexander H., 73, 102
Everett, Edward, 90, 133
Exposition and Protest, 116

Federalist party, 22, 66, 76, 81
Federation of Central America, 57,
    104
Ferdinand VII, King of Spain, 52–53
Fielding, Henry, 83
Fletcher v. Peck, 40
Florida, 54–56, 64, 102
Floyd, John, 120
Foote, Samuel A., 116
Force, Peter, 122
France, 11, 23, 43, 59, 60, 136–37,
    142
Franklin, Benjamin, 5, 6, 14, 16, 18,
    89, 144
Frazier, Mary, 20–22, 27
Frederick the Great, 19
Frederick Wilhelm II, King of Prussia,
    31
Frederick Wilhelm III, King of
    Prussia, 31
Free Soil party, 138

"gag" resolution, 137–45
Gaines, General Edmund Pendleton,
    93–94, 95
Gallatin, Albert, 43–47, 48–49, 53,
    67, 106, 107
Gambier, Admiral Lord, 45–47
Garrison, William Lloyd, 139
Genêt, Edmund, 23, 24
George Washington University, 85
Giusta, Antoine, 88
Godfrey, Martha, 118–19
Goulburn, Henry, 45–47
Great Britain, 5, 11, 23, 26, 42–43,
    45–47, 51–54, 58–61, 104–8,
    113, 142
Green, Duff, 119, 123, 126–27, 128

Hall, Joseph E., 67
Hamilton, Alexander, 22, 23, 81
Hammond, Charles, 123–24

Hammond, James H., 139
Hanseatic League, 104
Harrisburg Convention, 113
Harrison, General William Henry,
    115, 149
Harvard College, 12, 17, 19–20, 39,
    40, 90, 135
Hayne, Robert Y., 70–71, 83
Hellen, Mary, 117–18
Hellen, Walter, 36
Hill, Isaac, 118–19
Holland, 14, 25
Holmes, John, 83, 106
Holy Alliance, 52, 59–60
Hopkinson, Joseph, 67
Hoskisson, William, 106, 107
Hughes, Christopher, 105
Humphreys, David, 24

Indians, 54, 89–100, 137, 138,
    162
Industrial Revolution, 112
Ingham, Samuel, 120
Intolerable Acts, 5

Jackson, Andrew: and annexation of
    Texas, 143–44; and election of
    1824–25, 64, 74; and election of
    1828, 120–29; and foreign policy,
    136–37; as military leader, 46–47,
    54–55, 91; as president, 132–34,
    136; as presidential candidate,
    64–65, 67, 118–29; attacks JQA's
    administration, 74; defeat for
    president, 73; denounces Adams-
    Clay alliance, 74; dies, 154;
    elected to Senate, 64–65; opinion
    of JQA, 141; and patronage, 109;
    resigns from Senate, 74; seizes
    Florida, 54–55, 56
Jackson, Rachel, 119, 128
Jay, John, 14, 25
Jay Treaty, 26, 29, 31
Jefferson, Thomas, 5, 14, 16, 17, 18,
    22–23, 29, 32, 36, 37, 51, 59, 61,
    63, 89–90
Johnson, Catherine Nuth (mother-in-
    law), 26–27
Johnson, Joshua (father-in-law), 26,
    27–28, 29

King, Rufus, 39, 76
Kingdom of the Two Sicilies, 11

Land Act of 1820, 86
Lafayette, General, 89
Laurens, Henry, 14
League of Armed Neutrality, 11
Lee, Arthur, 5
Leopard, HMS, 38
Letcher, Robert, 69
Lincoln, Enoch, 103–4
Liverpool, Lord, 48
Livingston, Robert R., 35–36
Louisiana Purchase, 35–36, 54, 55, 56, 103, 120
Luzerne, Chevalier de la, 7

McIntosh, Chilly, 92
McIntosh, Chief William, 91–92
McKenney, Thomas L., 96
McLane, Louis, 71, 132
McLean, John, 63, 76, 77, 109
Macon, Nathaniel, 67, 68
Madison, James, 39–40, 41–43, 44, 54, 59, 61, 63, 85
Manifest Destiny, 44, 152
Mann, Horace, 90
Marbois, Barbé, 7
Marks, William, 121
Marshall, John, 76
Meriwether, James, 91, 92
Mexican War, 153–54
Mexico, 55, 57, 102–3, 104, 141–42, 143, 153–54
Monroe Doctrine, 50, 57–61
Monroe, Elizabeth, 62
Monroe, James, 24, 63, 75; as president, 48–49, 54–61; relations with JQA, 51, 55–56; as secretary of state, 46–47
Morgan, William, 125

Nagel, Paul, 15, 54
National Republican party, 84, 114, 119–29
National Road, 85–86
Netherlands, 26, 28
Neuville, Baron Jean-Guillame, 57
Nova Scotia, 16
Nullification controversy, 116, 133, 134

Obregón, Pable, 82–83
Onís, Luis de, 55–56, 57

Oregon, 152–53
O'Sullivan, John L., 152
Otis, Harrison Gray, 34, 39

Paine, Thomas, 22
Panama Congress, 78–79, 82–84, 102, 107, 120
Panic of 1819, 113
Panic of 1837, 149
Parsons, Lynn Hudson, 53
Parson, Theophilus, 20
Patton, John Mercer, 143
Peabody, Elizabeth, 40
Peabody, Stephen, 40
Peru, 57
Pennsylvania Society for the Promotion of Manufactures, 113
Pickering, Timothy, 35, 39, 135
Pinckney, Charles Cotesworth, 39
Pinckney, Henry R., 140
Pinckney, Thomas, 24, 26
Plumer, William, 36, 63, 68
Poinsett, Joel, 103
Polk, James K., 139, 151–53
Portugal, 11
Prussia, 11, 26, 29–32, 45, 104
Puerto Rico, 102

Quasi-War with France, 31
Quincy, John (great grandfather), 2
Quakers, 137

Randolph, Edmund, 25
Randolph, John, 73, 82, 83–84, 111, 120
Republican party, 22–23, 84
Rice, Nathan, 4
Richardson, Joseph, 132
"Right of petition," 138, 139, 143–45
Ritchie, Thomas 84
Rives, William C., 125
Robards, Lewis, 119
Rochester, William R., 82
Rush, Richard, 51–52, 53, 59, 76, 125
Rush-Bagot Agreement, 48, 52
Russell, Jonathan, 44, 66, 118, 135
Russia, 11, 13, 17–18, 40, 41–44, 59–60, 118–19, 153

St. Petersburg, 11–12, 13, 41
Salazar, José Maria, 82–83

Sanford, Nathan, 68
Scott, John, 71
Second Great Awakening, 137
Second National Bank of the United
    States, 133–34
Seminole Indians, 54, 91, 125
Sergeant, John, 82
Shaw, Reverend Joseph, 19
Short, William, 24
Silsbee, Nathaniel, 116
Slavery, 53, 77, 151
Smith, Elizabeth Quincy
    (grandmother), 2
Smith, Samuel, 36, 108
Smith, William (grandfather), 2
Smith, Colonel William (brother-in-
    law), 33
Smith, William Steuben, 41
Smithson, James, 144
Smyth, Alexander, 120
South America, 52–53, 57–61
Spain, 11, 28, 52–53, 55–56
Southard, Samuel, 75–76
Stevenson, Andrew, 110
Stockholm, 13–14
Story, Associate Justice Joseph, 64,
    147, 148
Sweden, 11, 31

Taney, Chief Justice Roger B., 148
Tappan, Lewis, 147, 149
Tariff of 1828, 112–16
Tariff of 1832, 133
Tariff of 1833 (Compromise), 134
Taylor, General Zachary, 153
Tazewell, Littleton W., 116
Texas, 55, 56, 102–3, 141–42,
    151–53
Thaxter, James, 4, 5, 7, 13
Thomas Jesse, 115
Thompson, Associate Justice Smith,
    147
Tom Jones, 83
Treaty of Fort Michel, 99
Treaty of Ghent, 44–47, 52, 91
Treaty of Indian Springs, 91–94, 95,
    97, 98
Treaty of Washington, 97, 98, 99,
    100

Troup, Governor George, 92–100
Turner, Nat, 137, 139
Tuyll, Baron Von, 59, 88
Twelfth Amendment, 37
Tyler, John, 115, 149, 151–52

University of Leyden, 10, 13, 15,
    17

Van Buren, Martin: and Adams-Clay
    alliance, 71; and *Amistad* case,
    147; as president, 144; Crawford's
    manager, 65, 66–67, 72, 73; and
    Free Soil party, 138, leads
    opposition to JQA's
    administration, 81–84, 108,
    110–11, 138; and Tariff of 1828,
    113–16; and Texas, 143
Van Rensselaer, Stephen, 72–73
Vesey, Denmark, 137, 139

War of 1812, 42–47, 50, 64, 85, 91,
    112
Warfield, Henry R., 71, 72
Warren, Dr. Joseph, 2
Washington, George, 14, 23, 24, 26,
    59, 63, 82
Waterhouse, Benjamin, 10
Webster, Daniel, 71, 72, 90, 106, 110,
    115, 124, 135, 136, 155
Webster-Ashburton Treaty, 104
Wellington, Duke of, Arthur
    Wellesley, 45, 46–47
West Indian dispute, 104–8
West Point, 79
Whig party, 134, 136–37, 149–50,
    152
Willard, Joseph, 19
Willey, Calvin, 116
Wilmot, David, 154
Wirt, William, 55, 76, 78, 133
Workingmen's party, 126
Wright, Silas, Jr., 116

XYZ Affair, 31

Yoholo, Opothle, 94, 96–97

ABOUT THE AUTHOR

Robert V. Remini is Professor Emeritus of History and the Humanities at the University of Illinois at Chicago. Called the foremost Jacksonian scholar of our time by the *New York Times*, he is the recipient of a National Book Award. His most recent book is *Andrew Jackson and His Indian Wars*.